Acolyte Leader's Resource Guide

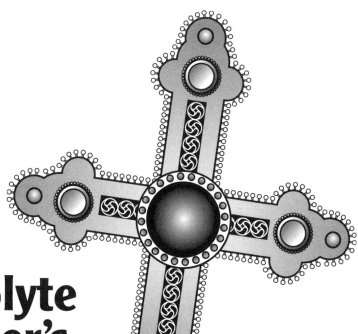

Acolyte
Leader's
Resource
Guide

Donna H. Barthle

MOREHOUSE PUBLISHING

An imprint of Church Publishing Incorporated
Harrisburg—New York

Morehouse Publishing
4775 Linglestown Road
Harrisburg, PA 17112

Morehouse Publishing is an imprint of Church Publishing Incorporated

Graphic design by Wesley Hoke

Library of Congress Cataloging-in-Publication Data

Barthle, Donna H.
  The acolyte leader's resource guide / Donna H. Barthle
      p. cm
Includes bibliographical references.
  ISBN 10 : 0-0-8192-1937-1 (pbk.)
  ISBN 13 : 978-0-8192-1937-4 (pbk.)
  1. Acolytes—Episcopal Church. 2. Episcopal Church—Liturgy. I. Title
  BX5948.B367   2003
  264'.03—dc21   2003001331

Printed in the United States of America

07   08   09   6   5   4   3

Table of Contents

Dedication

For my loving husband who sat alone in the pews for many years while I checked acolytes, rehearsed acolytes, and occasionally filled in for a missing acolyte, and during a shortage of servers one year, even learned to serve the altar—and found he enjoyed it.

Acknowledgments

My thanks to the many acolyte leaders, both ordained and lay, who freely shared their knowledge, parish traditions, and even frustrations with me to help prepare this book.

I am particularly grateful to the "pros" who shared their knowledge, advice, tips, and secrets. Stephen Lott, verger of the National Cathedral, kindly shared his knowledge and expert advice on processions and managing special services. Pastor Belvin Brummett, pastor of the Lutheran Church in Bowie, Texas, contributed his insight and knowledge of acolyte history as well as perspective on acolytes in different denominations. The Reverend Andrew Sherman, rector of The Episcopal Memorial Church of the Prince of Peace, Gettysburg, Pennsylvania, shared encouragement as well as his own references on liturgy and then graciously reviewed my interpretation of them.

A special thanks to the Reverend Bonnie Vandelinder, professor and librarian of the Lutheran Seminary, Gettysburg, Pennsylvania, and associate priest of the Prince of Peace Church, for sharing her encouragement, suggestions, and knowledge of vestments, liturgy, traditions, and all things Episcopalian.

Introduction

At the 1999 Annual Acolyte Festival at the National Cathedral, the bishop asked, "Who presents these acolytes for service at the altar of our Lord?" Acolyte leaders and priests from across America rose to their feet.

"We do," came the resounding reply.

We are the acolyte leaders, masters, supervisors, or subdeacons. Supervising and training acolytes and managing the program may be part of our duties as lay members of the parish, or as priests, deacons, or vergers. The title and exact content of the job varies from parish to parish depending on the size of the parish, its traditions, and the outlook of the rector or bishop.

However, there are basic duties and tenets grounded in history, tradition, and simple necessity that are common to us all. We share a common history. We recruit new acolytes, train and encourage them, schedule, and supervise the result. When the Sunday service is over and the last candle has been extinguished, we still have to plan and coordinate acolyte involvement in special services; we need to plan budgets and prepare reports.

Taking into account the minor and sometimes major differences between parishes, this book is designed as both a guide for new leaders and a resource for old hands. The chapter recounting a short history of the acolyte ministry specifically addresses some of those differences, as does the chapter describing the equipment and vestments you might expect to see in parishes, even if not your own. Included are detailed descriptions of traditional acolyte duties, along with service details that may help you better understand why we do the things we do.

The worksheets, checklists, forms, rosters, and letters included in this book are simply guides to use in developing your own management and administrative tools. These tools help shorten the time necessary for routine tasks and let you get back to the more important and rewarding part of your job—helping prepare young people and adults to serve at the altar of our Lord.

The Acolyte Leader's Resource Guide is a companion to The Parish Acolyte

Guide, also published by Morehouse Publishing. The Parish Acolyte Guide was developed for individual acolytes and contains a welcome letter, a short history of the acolyte ministry, a chapter describing equipment and vestments, and chapters detailing the responsibilities of the torchbearer, crucifer, server, and other acolyte positions. Since no one book can possibly reflect the different procedures for every parish, space has been left in each section for acolytes to fill in the particulars and the cues used in your own parish.

Managing the acolyte program can be a very real joy. This book is the result of my own learning experience, as well as that of acolyte leaders across the country. Most of us learned the hard way. We offer you our collected basic knowledge and resources to help build or refine your parish program into the joy that it should be for you and for your parish.

And finally, from the Form of Commitment to Christian Service in the Book of Common Prayer, I offer you this prayer:

"May the Holy Spirit guide and strengthen you, that in this, and in all things, you may do God's will in the service of the Kingdom of his Christ. Amen."

Peace,

Donna H. Barthle
Gettysburg, Pennsylvania
January 2, 2003

Chapter 1
A Short History of the Acolyte Ministry

The ministry of acolytes exists at the heart of our worship services. The ministry itself, the vestments, the titles, and the duties they perform in assisting a priest to prepare for the mystery that is the Holy Eucharist are directly tied to almost two thousand years of history. Borrowing from an old expression—you can't know where you're going, if you don't know where you've been.

The term acolyte comes from the Greek word *akolouthos*, meaning "follower" or "attendant." Although some people believe that the history of acolytes traces back to Samuel in the Old Testament, the first written historical record of the term appears in a letter from Pope Cornelius to the Bishop of Antioch in the year 251 C.E. In this letter, the Pope lists the clergy of Rome, which included forty-two acolytes.

In the early history of the church, acolytes were one of four lower orders of the clergy. The primary purpose of the order was to prepare young men for the priesthood. Their duties included lighting and extinguishing candles, carrying candles in procession, taking charge of the alms basin, helping the priest prepare for the Eucharist, and generally fetching and carrying. References in early texts also reveal that some acolytes carried consecrated (or blessed) bread to other churches, took Communion to the sick and imprisoned, and helped prepare and examine candidates for Baptism or Confirmation.

Between the fifth and ninth centuries, in a series of ancient directions to the clergy known as the *Ordines Romani*, acolyte duties are described and include the information that acolytes led and organized processions preceding the Pope. In the same time period, we also see the predecessor of modern gospel processions as two acolytes carried candles to accompany the reader and ensure that he had enough light to see the text.

A favorite story concerns the acolyte Tarsicus. In the year 258 C.E., the Roman Emperor Valerian decreed that bishops and priests were to sacrifice to the Roman gods and were forbidden to hold services. The penalty for violation of this decree was death. While taking the consecrated bread from the Pope to churches in the city of Rome, Tarsicus was stopped by a group of soldiers who wanted to see what he was concealing. He refused to show them the sacred bread and was beaten to death on the spot.

The involvement of young people and teenagers in the ministry isn't apparent until the ninth century at the Synod of Mainz, where it was declared that every priest should have a cleric or a boy to read the lessons and assist him in the services. This changed three things in church history. First, young people were allowed to serve the altar. Second, the training of these assistants was left to the individual priest. And third, there was no requirement for these lay assistants to train for or eventually join the priesthood. This is apparently where the parallel ministry of altar boys emerged, although acolytes as an order of the church did not disappear.

After Martin Luther posted his 95 Theses on the door of the Palast Church in Wittenberg, Germany, in 1517, few references to acolytes are found, and the ministry may have declined, possibly as a reaction against all things "Roman." The history of acolytes is further confused by the breakaway of other denominations, especially the formation of the Anglican Church when Henry VIII of England split the English Church from the Church of Rome in 1531.

During the Oxford movement in the early 1830s, the Anglican Church began a slow return to more traditional practices, and the ministry of acolytes began to reappear. The ministry all but disappeared for a time in the Lutheran Church but has recently been revived and is steadily growing in popularity as lay involvement in the church increases. In the Roman Catholic Church, while altar boys and girls are firmly established in their slightly limited roles, the ministry of acolytes still exists today as a separate ministry.

Girls and women were admitted to this all male ministry in the late 1970s and early 1980s. Their admittance may have been, and probably was, influenced by the women's liberation movement and the ordination of women into the priesthood of the Episcopal Church in 1979 and in the Lutheran Church a few years earlier in the same decade. Another strong influence may have been shrinking family size and the resulting shortage of boys in the right age group. Whether of necessity or because of cultural rebellion, women and girls entered the ministry and were fully integrated by the 1990s in most Episcopal parishes. Most, although not all, Catholic parishes now also assign girls to serve on the altar.

Acolytes today remain servants of the altar. No matter the parish or even denominational differences, the primary duty of an acolyte is still to serve God and the Church, and to assist the priest in whatever way he or she needs or prefers. Electricity, instead of candles, now lights a very different altar than Christians of the year 251 C.E. were accustomed to seeing. Those same Christians might easily recognize however the humble figure at the foot of the altar dressed in cassock or alb and doing many of the same jobs as his or her predecessor of nearly two thousand years ago.

Chapter 2
Identifying Equipment and Vestments

Every vestment and piece of equipment on the altar has a specific purpose and a significance that in some cases goes back centuries, but in other cases, may be the result of practical invention in your specific parish. This discussion will touch on and briefly describe a broad range, although not all, of the vestments and equipment commonly used in parish churches. Every parish is a little different, and a comprehensive review would require an entire book.

Vestments for Acolytes, Priests, and Deacons

Acolytes wear one of two types of vestment, either the cassock and cotta or surplice, or the server's alb. Both serve to cover street clothes and help keep the attention of both the acolyte and the congregation on worship rather than on the latest fashion.

Cassock: A simple robe with a high split collar, fitted at the shoulders and sleeves and falling straight to the ankle with no elaborate tucks or gathers. It is usually worn with a surplice or cotta. The traditional color for acolyte cassocks is red, the color of celebration. The priest's cassock is most often black. The cassock was originally the outer garment worn by a priest.

Cassock, cotta, and alb with cincture.

Surplice or cotta: A loose fitting overgarment with bell sleeves. It is usually white and made of gathered material attached to a rounded or square yoke. A surplice or cotta is worn over the cassock. Acolytes and choir generally wear the shorter cotta. An acolyte's sleeves are often shortened to keep them from catching on vessels or equipment as the acolyte works. Priests most often wear the longer cathedral-length surplice with full-length sleeves. The historical purpose of a surplice or cotta was to keep the cassock clean during the working part of the service, which is why, in many parishes, the acolyte still performs any duties before the entry procession and after the exit procession without wearing the cotta.

Server's alb: A simple, long, loose-fitting robe with sleeves, with or without a hood. It is tied at the waist with a rope belt called a cincture. The alb is generally white or flax colored, although some parishes now use other colors. In monastic history, the alb was the simple clothing of religious orders. Priests may also wear an alb as a basic garment to cover street clothing under clerical vestments. Historically, the acolyte's vestments concealed or covered differences in social status, ensured that only relatively clean outer clothing was worn to approach the altar, and kept the wearer warm in unheated stone churches.

Cincture: This is the long rope belt tied around the waist of an alb. Acolytes usually tie this in a simple square or slipknot on the right side with the ends hanging fairly even. Priests also wear the cincture but tie it differently.

Pectoral cross or pendant: Many acolytes wear a cross of wood or metal or a pendant particular to their parish while serving the altar as a reminder to themselves and others of their duties. The server's cross is usually three to four inches in length and worn on a cord long enough so the cross hangs over the wearer's heart.

Chasuble: A chasuble is a priest's vestment worn for Eucharistic services. Similar to a poncho, it hangs from the shoulders, has no specific sleeves, and may be oval or rectangular. Depending on style, it may have a collar or cowl. If there is more than one priest at a service, the primary celebrant wears the chasuble. Historical accounts disagree as to the origin and symbolism behind both the chasuble and the stole but most include the fact that the chasuble designated the primary celebrant at the Eucharist and provided extra warmth. The usual colors match the church seasons, for example, green, white, blue, and red.

Stole: This is a priest's vestment worn for sacramental services. The stole is a long, narrow cloth worn draped around the neck and hanging loose from both shoulders to about the knees. It may or may not be color coded to match the colors of the altar hangings and the church seasons. Deacons also wear a stole when assisting with sacramental services, but deacons wear it across the chest and crossed or loosely knotted at the hip like a sash. As an alternative, deacons wearing a Byzantine stole wear it across the chest but cross or knot it at the shoulder with the longer, loose ends hanging at the front and back.

Cope: Also a priest's vestment, but unlike the chasuble, a cope looks more like a cape and closes in the front across the chest. Copes are often worn by bishops but may also be worn by priests, deacons, or the laity on special or festive occasions. They are generally quite elaborate.

Dalmatic: A dalmatic is a deacon's vestment generally worn over an alb for services. The color generally varies with the church seasons as do the chasuble and altar hangings. However, the deacon's vestment is more tailored than a chasuble and has sleeves.

On the Altar, You Will Find ...

Chalice and paten: The chalice is the cup used to hold the wine and water. The paten is a small plate used to hold the host bread during the Eucharist. You may hear the terms communion cup or common cup for the chalice and bread plate or tray instead of paten. The chalice and paten are usually a matched set and may be stored together under a veil on the altar (see description of veil below) before and during services. In some parishes, the chalice and paten are kept on the credence table until they are needed in the service and are returned there afterward.

Chalice, paten, service book, and gospel book on the altar

Gospel book: The book of gospel readings used during the service.

Candles: Candles, in general, represent the light of Christ in the world. The two larger candles on either edge of the altar are the eucharistic candles. On the left is the gospel candle (the gospel was traditionally read on that side of the church), and on the right is the epistle candle (the epistles or lessons were traditionally read on that side of the church). The Paschal candle, a large, decorated candle, generally in a separate stand, is used for the fifty days of Easter and for Baptisms, funerals, and other special occasions. The Paschal candle specifically represents the light of the risen Christ and is lighted for the first time each year during the Easter Vigil. Some parishes also use six additional candles, called service candles or office lights. These are lighted routinely for Morning Prayer and all other altar-based services. Office lights are most often used in churches where the altar is against the sanctuary wall or where a candle rail or shelf has been installed on the wall behind and above the altar. Other candles used in the service include Advent candles (usually in a wreath) and sanctuary lights (see below).

Service book: This is the prayer book used by the priest, which contains the service and rubrics (instructions for the priest) in print large enough to be read while conducting the service.

Cross or crucifix: On or above the altar, you will generally find a plain cross or crucifix (with a representation of the body of Christ) as a reminder that our faith is based on the life and resurrection of Christ.

Basic altar hangings: These usually include an altar cover in white linen or in the colors of the church seasons. If the cloth is in a color or fabric other than plain white linen, it may be called a "frontal." Lectern and pulpit hangings usually match the colors and symbols on the frontal.

Altar linens: The different linens can be confusing and for the most part the priest and altar guild will deal with them. But occasionally a replacement or extra piece of linen may be needed, and acolytes should be able to identify the basics without a great deal of fuss.

The "fair linen" is the long white, rectangular linen cloth on top of the altar cover.

A "purificator" is a small 12 by 12 inch linen napkin used to wipe the chalice after Communion that is folded in thirds and may have a small cross embroidered on its face.

The "corporal" is a larger napkin (about 20 by 20 inches) that the priest places on the fair linen under the chalice and paten while he or she prepares the Eucharist. It generally has a cross embroidered in the center or in one corner and is also folded in thirds.

The "pall" is a small (7 by 7 inches) stiff white linen-covered square placed over the chalice when it is not in use.

The "veil" covers the chalice, paten, and pall before and after Communion while those vessels are on the altar. The veil may be white linen but is usually in colors that match the frontal and other hangings. A veil is not used if the chalice and paten are kept on the credence table.

The "burse" is a 9 by 9 inch folder or pocket that holds the service linens. It may also match the altar hangings or be made of white linen.

On the Credence Table, You Will Find ...

The "credence table cover" is smaller than the fair linen and often has a 2-inch embroidered cross.

The "host box", also called a breadbox, is generally a small silver, gold, or ceramic box with a lid, and contains the wafers to be consecrated during the Eucharist. In place of a host box, a ciborium, which is shaped like a chalice with a lid, may be used.

The two cruets, which can be made of glass, crystal, or ceramic, contain wine in one and water in the other. For large services, a large silver or ceramic flagon may be used to hold the wine.

The lavabo bowl and a lavabo towel (rectangular, about 10 by 15 inches) are used for the ceremonial washing of the priest's hands before the Eucharist.
A second chalice covered by a purificator and pall may also be on the table if more than one chalice is needed for the service.

On the lower shelf or on a nearby table, you will usually find an alms basin and collection plates or baskets. The term "alms basin" actually applies to the large basin used to carry two or more stacked collection plates, however, the term may also be used to refer to the smaller basins or collection plates.

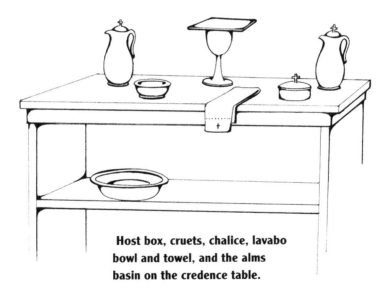

Host box, cruets, chalice, lavabo bowl and towel, and the alms basin on the credence table.

Other Equipment Acolytes Use

Torch or taper: Both terms refer to candles, generally wax or oil filled, that are carried in processions to light the processional cross or the path of a visiting dignitary. If the candle is mounted on a staff, it is usually referred to as a torch. If it is in a candleholder, it is usually referred to as a taper. The term taper may also refer to the thin wax-covered wick in the candle lighter. Both items are also used to refer to the acolyte who carries the candle.

Processional cross: This is a cross or crucifix mounted on a staff for processions. The processional cross, carried by a crucifer, generally leads the procession as a reminder that we are called to follow the cross. The entrance of the cross begins the formal worship service.

Sanctus bells: A group of four small bells attached to a single handle. Some parishes use a gong and mallet for the same purpose. The bells are used in many parishes to signal the celebration and presence of Christ in our midst during the Eucharist at the acclamation and at the elevation of the bread and wine. Long ago, when the services were conducted in Latin rather than in the language of the local population, the bells signaled the congregation at important moments in the service.

Sacristy bells: Sacristy bells are either a single bell or a set of three bells, usually attached to a cord and hung on the wall next to the door of the sacristy. The bells, usually rung by an acolyte, signal the entry of the clergy and the beginning of the service.

Thurible and boat: The thurible is a brass container designed to hold charcoal and incense. It usually has a chain attached to either its sides or a lid so that it may be safely carried in procession. The boat, a small container with a spoon and lid, is used to carry extra incense to be used during the service. Incense has been used since biblical times as both an offering to God and to visually represent our prayers rising to God. A third biblical use was to cleanse or purify offerings to God. The traditional offerings include the alms, bread and wine, and even ourselves (see Eucharistic prayers, page 336,

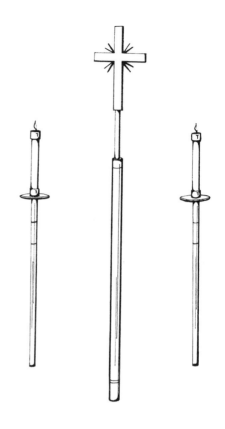

Torches and processional cross.

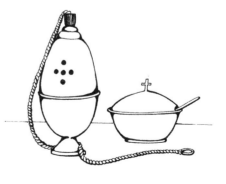

Thurible and boat with spoon.

BCP). Some churches today use incense routinely for eucharistic services. Some churches use it only for special occasions and others use it rarely, if at all.

Banners and flags: A banner is a cloth flag mounted horizontally instead of vertically so that its full face is always displayed. Banners display messages or symbols special to an occasion or to a particular group. The concept of banners goes back to the feudal period when each king or feudal lord had his family symbol or crest embroidered on banners hung from his castle walls and on smaller banners or flags carried with him as he traveled. Anyone approaching from a distance then knew whose forces controlled the castle, and those inside the castle could identify an approaching group before they were close enough to be a danger. Banners and flags (the cloth is vertical on the staff) are still used to identify many types of organizations. The Episcopal Church has its own specific flag (vertical like the U.S. flag), and many parishes have specific identifying banners.

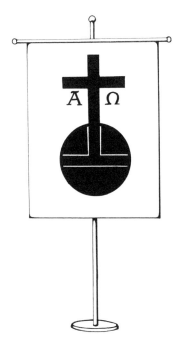

Banner and stand.

Inside the Sanctuary Rail

The aumbry or tabernacle: Either term may be used to refer to the cabinet or case used to store the reserved consecrated elements. Priests or lay ministers use the reserved elements when taking Communion to those who are sick or unable to attend the service. Acolytes are not normally asked to open the aumbry.

Sanctuary lamp: Close to the aumbry or tabernacle you may find a candle or oil lamp that burns at all times throughout the year. The light reminds us that Christ is present in the consecrated elements. The only time the sanctuary light is extinguished is after the Maundy Thursday service when the altar is stripped for Good Friday. It is relit after the Easter Vigil.

In the Nave

Baptismal font and holy water font: The baptismal font is a stand with a basin for holding water during a Baptism. The font can be made of marble in one piece and can be quite elaborate or as simple as a table and ceramic basin. The holy water font can be a separate stand with basin, or a small half-basin attached to the wall near the entry to the nave. Historically, baptismal fonts were placed in the back of the nave and close to the door as a reminder that it is through Baptism that we enter the Christian community. When entering the church, we are encouraged to dip a finger in the holy water and make the sign of the cross on our own forehead as a reminder of the promises made at our Baptism and renewed at our Confirmation.

Stations of the cross: A series of plaques placed at intervals on the walls of the nave tell the story of Jesus' journey to the crucifixion and resurrection. These are used mostly during Lent for a short service in which participants walk from station to station to hear a piece of the story at each and share prayers.

Other Items

Never be afraid to ask your priest (or a member of the altar guild) to explain the purpose and uses of vestments and equipment that you aren't sure about or don't recognize. The more you know and understand, the better job you can do as an acolyte. More information is also available in the books and websites listed in the Resources section on page 66.

Chapter 3
Acolyte Duties: What We Do and How We Do It

Acolytes perform a variety of duties that support the worship service and assist the priest to celebrate the Eucharist and guide worship. Some of those duties, and how they are performed, are age-old. Others have been adjusted to meet the needs of modern worship services, the traditions of the parish, and the particular priest celebrating and therefore in charge of the service. The descriptions provided below detail the more common methods and explain why traditional methods are still so often the standard.

Lighting and Tending the Altar Candles

One of the first duties of an acolyte is to light and tend the altar candles. The two eucharistic candles (with the gospel candle on the left as you face the altar and the epistle candle on the right), the service candles or office lights, the Advent wreath, and the individual hand candles for the congregation all have symbolic significance. The Paschal candle may also be used during the fifty days of Easter, for Baptisms, and for funerals. It represents the light of the risen Christ. If it is present, it takes precedence and is lighted first and extinguished last. If at all possible, the Paschal candle should actually be lit ahead of time, and then the eucharistic candles and service lights should be lit from it.

The altar candles should be lighted fifteen minutes before the formal beginning of the service. This is a time of meditation and preparation for those who have come to worship. To light the candles, an acolyte approaches the altar from inside the rail, carrying the lighter/snuffer, bows from the waist (this is considered a solemn bow) to reverence the altar, and then steps up to a point at which he or she can reach all the candles. If the Paschal candle is present, it is lighted first. Next, bringing the lighter to the outside edge of the altar, the acolyte lights the epistle candle and moves the lighter back off the edge of the altar. Moving the lighter around to the gospel side—*not* across the altar cloth—he or she repeats the process and lights the gospel candle. Moving the lighter directly across the altar risks dripping wax on the altar cloth. The acolyte then steps back and again reverences the altar before returning to the sacristy to put away the lighter/snuffer. As a reminder of the proper order, remember that, "the gospel candle never stands alone." Of the two eucharistic candles, the gospel candle is lighted last and extinguished first.

To extinguish the altar candles at the end of the service, the acolyte approaches the altar at a dignified pace, reverences with a solemn bow, steps up, and places the bell of the snuffer just over the follower (the brass cap on the top of the candle) on the gospel candle and counts to three. This should be enough time for the flame to extinguish. Pressing the bell down too far presses the wick into the wax and makes the candle difficult to light again without trimming. He or she repeats the process (again being careful not to move the snuffer directly across the altar cloth) to extinguish the epistle candle. The Paschal candle is extinguished last. The acolyte then steps back and reverences the altar before retreating to the sacristy.

Order for Lighting Altar Candles
Move the lighter off the altar—not across the altar.
When the Paschal candle is present, it is lit first.

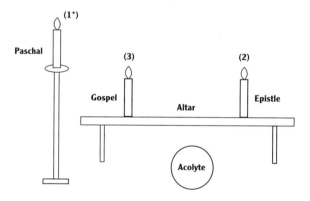

Order for Extinguishing Altar Candles

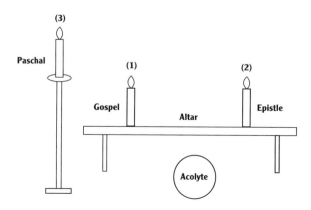

   Many churches also use six additional service candles or office lights on the altar or on a special rail or shelf behind and above the altar. They are often arranged in candelabrum or in separate holders with three candles on each side of the altar. These are lit for Morning Prayer and other altar-based liturgies as well as eucharistic services. Lighting the service candles, but not the eucharistic candles, signals the congregation that the service will not include the Eucharist. If the eucharistic candles are also lit, Eucharist will be included. The service candles are lit and extinguished after the eucharistic candles. To remember the order for lighting these, think of a set of curtains: Beginning on the epistle side, start at the center of the altar and move to the outside as if you were drawing back a curtain. Then move to the gospel side, and again move from the center to the outside. Conversely, at the end of the service, close the curtains by starting from the outside of the gospel side and then moving toward the center. Then repeat for the other side. The order of lighting is shown below.

Order for Lighting Altar Candles with Office Lights
*The Paschal candle is used only for special occasions.

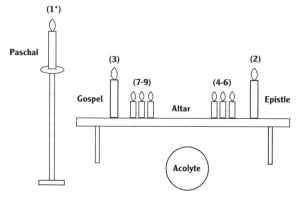

Order for Extinguishing Altar Candles with Office Lights
*When it is present, the Paschal candle is extinguished last.

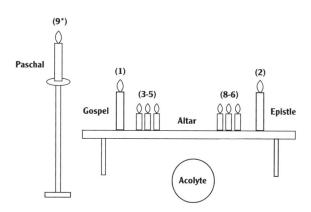

If hand candles or congregational candles are used, from one to four acolytes light their own hand candles from either the Paschal candle or the eucharistic candles and proceed down the church aisles, lighting the hand candles of the first person in each pew and asking them to light the candle of the person sitting next to him or her. In this way, we share the light of Christ. To minimize wax drips on pew covers, the acolyte should hold his or her candle upright while the other person tips their unlit candle to catch the flame.

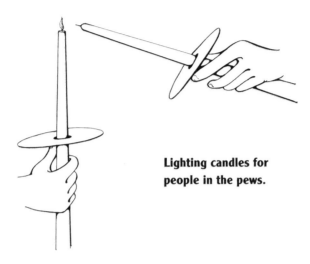

Lighting candles for people in the pews.

Carrying Candles in Processions

Candles carried in procession are generally set in stands at prearranged positions close to the altar (those with staffs) or on the altar table itself (those in candle holders). If the candles are used to illuminate the cross or crucifix that leads the procession into the sanctuary, they should be carried with the flames even with each other and just under the cross piece on the processional cross.

Carrying a processional torch (on a staff) requires practiced balance. The torch is lifted with two hands. The lower hand holds the staff at belt level braced against the waist. The other hand grips the staff just below the bridge of the acolyte's nose. The elbow should be parallel to the floor. When torchbearers (the acolyte carrying the lighted candle can also be called a torch or taper) move together, they should use opposite upper arms so as not to elbow each other. The torch should be pulled in close to the body for maximum stability. This also keeps the candle or taper upright and level. Processional tapers or torches usually have drip plates but can still drip hot wax on vestments or in the acolyte's hair if not kept steady. Even the oil-filled candles often used in place of tapers need to be kept strictly upright.

An easy way to make sure that processional tapers or torches are at the same height is to have the two torchbearers face each other, adjust the drip plates on the processional torches to the same height, and then turn, shoulder to shoulder, to face forward. Either the crucifer or the torchbearers themselves light the processional tapers or torches five minutes before the procession begins.

Leading Processions

A procession signals a formal beginning and ending to our services, but it also helps create an atmosphere of celebration and joy for worship. It is normally led by an acolyte carrying a cross or crucifix, which reminds us of our purpose in gathering. A procession can simply consist of an acolyte carrying a processional cross, the lay eucharistic ministers (LEMs) or chalice bearers, and the priest, or be as complex as a full festival procession that might include the congre-

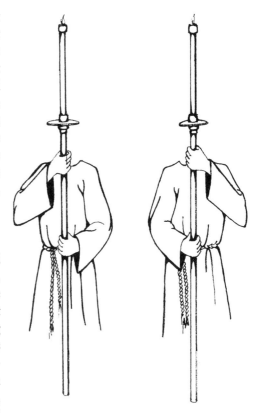

Two torchbearers side by side with hands in proper position.

gation depending on the occasion and the traditions of the parish. Organizing processions, including order of precedence, cues for special processions, and so forth, is discussed in depth in Chapter 6; however, basic instructions include the following.

The basic method for carrying or balancing the processional cross is to lift it with two hands, like the torch, using the bottom hand for stability against the acolyte's waist and with the top hand placed just under the bridge of the nose. The staff should be pulled in against the body. The acolyte's wrist should be turned in with the elbow parallel to the floor. The old tradition of turning the wrist outward may cause strain to a young person's shoulder.

After checking to be sure that all participants are present and lined up properly, the crucifer starts the procession at a prearranged cue, for example, the second verse of the entry hymn. He or she sets a stately, unhurried pace while leading the procession to the altar. The ideal is to have the procession end with everyone at his or her place in the sanctuary and ready to begin the service by the middle of the last verse. The exit procession also generally begins at a prearranged cue, such as the beginning of the recessional hymn. At that point, the crucifer gets the processional cross and waits with the torchbearers at a prearranged point, such as the center front of the altar. As the other service participants join them, they turn and move down the aisle.

After the exit or retiring procession, the crucifer proceeds back up a side aisle or service entrance to extinguish the altar candles before the final blessing. In some parishes, the torchbearers extinguish the altar candles.

Presenting the Gospel

How the gospel procession is handled in a particular parish depends to a great extent on whether or not the parish has a deacon. It is a deacon's prerogative to read and carry the gospels. The deacon may carry the book him or her-

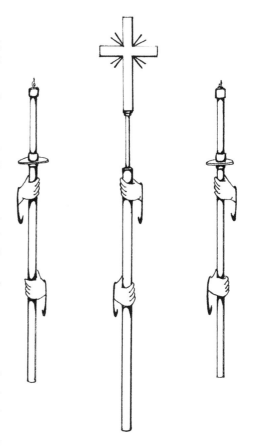

Processional cross and torches.

self to the center of the church or other designated location for the gospel proclamation and hand it to the acolyte to hold for the reading or have the acolyte carry and hold the gospel book. Alternatively, the crucifer and torchbearers may lead the deacon while he or she carries the Gospels and then reads and returns the book to the altar.

However, in parishes without a deacon, a formal gospel procession is generally handled in the following way. The acolyte, usually the crucifer, picks up the gospel book from the altar at whatever cue has been established (for example, the last verse of the gospel hymn) and carries it to the center of the church or a designated place in the particular church. The cross on the front cover should always face forward so it is visible to the congregation. If torchbearers are included in the procession, they follow the crucifer and position themselves either beside or behind the crucifer, depending on the space available. When holding the book for the priest or deacon to read, the crucifer or acolyte braces his or her elbows against his or her rib cage with the book resting on outstretched forearms. When the priest or deacon opens the book and rests it on the acolyte's arms, the acolyte curls his or her fingers up and over the bottom edge of the book to hold the page. The priest or deacon reads the gospel selection for the day, raises the book, closes it, and lays it back in the acolyte's arms. The priest or deacon then steps aside to allow the crucifer and torchbearers to lead the procession back to the altar. For more detail, see Chapter 6.

Handling the Alms Basin and Collection Plates

In most parishes the alms basin and/or collection plates are kept on the lower shelf of the credence table or someplace nearby. The acolyte brings the plates around and to the front of the altar to the ushers at the appropriate moment in the service (that is, after the offertory sentences). In exchange, the ushers generally give the acolyte the count of communicants present so that the clergy can prepare sufficiently for the Eucharist. While the collection is going on, the acolyte helps the priest or deacon prepare the altar. After the altar is prepared, the acolyte returns to the front of the altar and receives the basins from the ushers.

The collection plates and alms basin should be carried around the altar (not handed across) to the priest to be presented. If the priest returns the basin to the acolyte, it should be returned to the lower shelf of the credence table before the acolyte returns to his or her seat and the service continues. In some parishes, the alms basin remains on the altar throughout the Eucharist, and the acolyte returns them to the credence table after Communion.

Preparing for the Eucharist

At whatever cue is agreed on beforehand (generally after the offertory sentences), the acolyte server helps prepare the altar for the Eucharist. For large services, a second chalice may be needed. This may be delivered to the altar before the collection plates are given to the ushers or later after the fraction. If the ushers or other members of the congregation bring forward the gifts (bread and wine), the server takes the alms basins to the rail, and with one hand, offers the plates and takes the ciborium or breadbox and places it on the credence table. He or she then returns to the rail and takes the water and wine to the credence table. In simpler services, the bread and wine are already set out on the credence table.

There are a few general rules for the acolyte to remember in serving the altar. First, lids and stoppers are left on the credence table. Second, silent language is generally used on the altar. Once a server understands what is needed to prepare for Communion, speech is replaced with the unspoken language of the altar. For example, when the priest is finished with the breadbox or wine and water, he or she bows slightly to the acolyte in an unspoken gesture that says, "I'm done, thank you." The server bows in return to say, "You're welcome." If an acolyte forgets something, the priest will often point and then open his or her hands in a palms-up gesture that says, "I need that now." Acolytes often use the same open-hand gesture to say, "I'll hold that for you."

After the collection plates have been passed to the ushers, the server or acolyte helps to prepare the table by bringing the bread, wine, and water to the altar. Either a priest or deacon may prepare the table for the Eucharist.

To present the bread, the acolyte removes the lid from the breadbox and brings the box from the credence table to the priest or deacon. If the acolyte has been given the number of communicants, he or she gives that number to the priest and holds out the breadbox. The priest may or may not take it from the acolyte's hands, so the acolyte should hold the box with two hands near the bottom. The priest takes what he or she needs from the box and then bows to show he or she is finished. The acolyte bows in acknowledgment and returns the box to the credence table and replaces the lid.

Next the acolyte carries both the water and wine cruets to the altar. Because the wine will be poured first, that cruet should be in the acolyte's right hand with the handle facing the priest or deacon. A well-trained acolyte always gives with the right hand and takes items back with the left hand. As soon as the priest takes the wine cruet, the acolyte moves the water to the right hand. As soon as the priest is finished with the wine, the acolyte holds out the left hand to take it, immediately offers the water, and then moves the wine to the right so as to leave the left hand free. The circular method of handling the cruets is age-old and may sound fussy but is actually simple and limits the possibility of accidents while handling delicate articles. Because both acolyte and priest know what to expect, their movements are smooth and efficient. The priest may prefer to keep the wine cruet or a flagon (for larger services) on the altar rather than returning it to the acolyte.

After returning the cruet(s) to the credence table, the acolyte picks up the lavabo bowl in the left hand, drapes the small towel over the left wrist and forearm, picks up the water cruet (by the handle) with the right hand, and returns to the altar to assist the primary celebrant in washing his or her hands. The celebrating priest may or may not be the same person who set the altar. The acolyte holds out the bowl, the priest places his or her fingers over the bowl, and the acolyte pours water over them. The acolyte then holds out his or her forearm to offer the towel and keeps the arm there until the celebrant replaces the towel. The lavabo bowl, towel, and cruet are then returned to the credence table, and the stoppers to the cruets are replaced before the acolyte goes to the front of the altar to receive the alms.

Fetching and Carrying

The usual chores and duties acolytes perform are listed above; however, acolytes are servants of God and his Church and specifically of the priest. Their job may include almost anything needed to make the worship service flow more smoothly. During a Baptism, for example, an acolyte will often hold the priest's prayer book, bring out the water at the appropriate moment, hand out baptismal certificates, light the baptismal candles from the Paschal candle, and remove extra tables or items after the Baptism.

Answering the Priest and Being a Good Example

During the low Middle Ages when the language of the church services was changed from the language of the people (in that case Greek) to Latin, acolytes were often chosen because they had some grasp of that language and could answer the priest with the responses of the people during the Mass. Today, services are held in the language of the local population, but worship leaders may still rely upon acolytes to begin the congregational responses. Visitors especially watch the acolytes to know when to kneel, sit, or stand during the service. It is important that acolytes participate in the service and provide that leadership.

To provide a good example for the congregation, acolytes should do the following:

- During those parts of the service when the priest is seated, wait for the priest to sit first.
- Follow the priest's example of when to cross one's self or bow (for example, at the name of Christ).
- When crossing in front of or behind the altar, always reverence the cross (either bow from the waist or genuflect). The exception to this rule is when carrying something, for example, a torch or processional cross.
- When kneeling, keep the back straight instead of leaning back against the chairs.
- Stand and sit up straight, and pay attention to the service.
- When hands are not directly in use, keep them folded at or slightly above waist level.
- Treat duties with reverence and respect, and remember at all times whom they serve.

When all members of the altar party project an attitude of reverence, the congregation responds and the service is enriched for all.

Which Acolyte Does What

For simple services, one acolyte alone may provide all the support necessary and perform the duties attributed as noted above to the crucifer and the server. At other services, three, four, or more acolytes may be needed. At services in which several acolytes serve, the duties are usually parceled out between them, based partly on traditional divisions but also on the number of acolytes available and their level of experience. See the next chapter for a discussion of traditional acolyte positions and division of responsibilities.

Duties and Items Reserved for the Clergy

There are some duties as well as items on the altar that only a priest or specially trained member of the laity traditionally handle. For example, only a priest or deacon generally reads the gospel for a eucharistic service. Along the same lines, only a priest, deacon, or chalice bearer normally handles consecrated elements (bread and wine). Another job reserved for the clergy includes censing the altar. The deacon or a thurifer may be asked to cense the clergy and the congregation, but only the priest or bishop will cense the altar. Individual parish priests may reserve other duties and articles as well. The altar of our Lord is a holy place. In order to serve there with reverence, it is important for acolytes to know and understand what they may and may not do and touch.

Everyone Makes Mistakes

Last, it's important to understand that we all make mistakes. At an acolyte festival in 1997, a visiting bishop told about his own worst moment as an acolyte. On an Easter Sunday, he was carrying several very full alms basins to the priest to be presented when he tripped on the altar steps. Bills, checks, and envelopes fluttered to the floor while quarters, dimes, and nickels rolled down the aisles and under the pews. Half the congregation got on their hands and knees to help retrieve the money. It was every acolyte's nightmare.

Once we finished laughing, the bishop told us that if God did not smite him for that, there wasn't much we could do that would bring down the Almighty's wrath.

Mistakes and accidents happen to everyone. The important lesson is to respond to our own and the mistakes of others with grace (not hysteria), to learn from them, and to try not to make the same mistake twice.

Chapter 4
Acolyte Positions and Duties

At first glance, the most apparent reason for dividing acolyte duties into different positions is to allow more people to be directly involved in supporting the worship service. While this does have advantages, it's not the only reason. Dividing acolyte duties into different established positions allows leaders to train acolytes beginning with the simpler tasks and then moving on to more complex tasks and greater responsibility.

Established positions also allow for continuity in the service itself. Each member of the service team knows exactly what's expected of him or her. And from this basic level of service support, minor changes for special services such as a Baptism, or even major changes such as for a festival service, can then be added with less effort.

Because diversity is the nature of our particular ministry, no one book can accurately describe the exact division of duties for acolyte positions in every parish. The traditional positions used in most parishes follow.

Torchbearers

The torchbearer, or taper or torch, as it is referred to in some parishes, carries a candle, called a torch or taper, in processions. The purpose of carrying lighted candles is to highlight the processional cross, the gospel reading, or a visiting bishop or other distinguished person. To truly understand the historical importance of this simple duty, imagine for a moment the churches and cathedrals of only a century ago. The sanctuaries were large and open, dimmed by stained-glass windows and unlit by electric lights. Even on a sunny day, the interiors tended to be gloomy and dark.

Most traditions have practical roots. The torchbearers—there are always two of them—still provide extra light and make the procession special and highly visible for the gathered worshipers. Torchbearers are also often responsible for lighting the hand candles for the congregation during candlelight services and for positioning or removing furniture or other items, such as the bishop's chair used during Confirmation.

The Crucifer

The crucifer's basic job is to carry the cross in processions. His or her duties expand from this point, depending on the parish. He or she may also tend the altar candles before and after the service, carry the gospel book in procession, and hold it for the reading. The crucifer may also supervise the torchbearers. This responsibility includes making sure the torchbearers arrive on time, finding replacements if they don't arrive for the service, making sure they are properly vested and know their cues, and have any additional instructions necessary for changes in the service. Since the crucifer generally leads processions (except when a thurifer is present), he or she also reviews any changes in the cues beforehand and makes sure those involved know what to expect.

In some parishes, the crucifer is the senior acolyte on duty and supervises the acolyte service team. In other parishes, the server is the senior acolyte. The crucifer can also double as the server.

The Server

The server helps the priest prepare for the holy Eucharist by bringing the bread, wine, and water, handling the alms basins, helping with the lavabo, and ringing the Sanctus bells during the Eucharist. If a crucifer is not assigned, the server also tends the altar candles before and after the service. The server is the servant or assistant to the celebrant and may be asked to fetch extra items from the sacristy, hold the priest's prayer book, read lessons as needed, or perform other chores. In many parishes, the server is the senior acolyte. He or she checks with the priest for changes before the service and shares that information with the team, replaces missing or late acolytes as needed, and generally supervises the acolyte team. The server can also double as the crucifer.

The Thurifer

The thurifer carries the thurible in processions and for the Eucharist. The thurifer is responsible for learning how the thurible or censer works, lighting charcoal (and keeping it lit), and learning the rhythms or swings used in processions and to cense the congregation. The priest will cense the altar, but the acolyte may be asked to cense the priest, altar party, or congregation. Incense is used routinely in some parishes, but in other parishes is used only for a high or festival mass. It is generally an advanced duty learned by more experienced senior acolytes.

The Banner Bearer

The banner represents the parish or possibly a particular philosophy or event. For example, a parish may have a banner that bears its name and a symbol particular to it but may also have banners representing special occasions, such as Pentecost. The banner bearer carries the banner and, by extension, represents the congregation.

Some parishes prefer to have the banner carried by a different person every time. This presents the acolyte leader with a special training challenge. The one-page job description in the Parish Acolyte's Guide makes a good training aid for parish members.

The Book Bearer

The book bearer (or book) carries the gospel book in procession. A priest, deacon, or acolyte may perform this job. This position is most often seen in festival or special services such as an ordination or other high mass. Processing the gospel book reminds the congregation of the importance of the gospel to our service and in our lives. A deacon or priest carries the gospel book elevated or raised at about eye level. Acolytes carry the book laid on both forearms with the fingers curled over the bottom edge.

The Boat Bearer

The boat bearer (or boat) carries the boat in procession. The boat is the small container with a lid and spoon that holds the incense for the thurible or censer. Since the incense is an offering, it is carried with two hands at waist level. If a special acolyte is not assigned for this duty, the server usually carries the boat.

The Senior Acolyte

The duties of the senior acolyte may be and often are combined with the duties of either the crucifer or server.

The term "senior acolyte" may also be used to refer to an acolyte in charge of managing a festival or special service, or it may refer more generally to the more experienced acolytes in the parish. Senior acolytes are usually trained in all the acolyte positions used by that parish, from torchbearer to crucifer and server, to thurifer and banner bearer. The senior acolyte for a festival or other special service will usually be involved from the planning phase, through rehearsal, to setting out seat markers and hand candles, and with rehearsing the serving acolytes in preparing for the service.

The Bishop's Server

Many bishops travel with their own chaplain to act as server, although others do not. In that case, the parish may provide an associate priest, deacon, or a senior acolyte server to assist the bishop. The server (priest, deacon, or acolyte) should meet the bishop at the door, and after being introduced by the parish priest, offer his or her services and ask specifically how he or she may serve. This may include carrying the bishop's staff or crook during processions, hanging the bishop's cope and miter in the sacristy during the service when they're not needed, and holding the bishop's prayer book or the small container of oil during the service if he or she needs to use both hands (for example, for the laying on of hands at Confirmation). The regular server usually assists the deacon or priest to prepare the table for the Eucharist. But since the bishop will most likely be the celebrant, the bishop's server assists him or her with the lavabo. After the final Communion prayer, the bishop's server usually retrieves the bishop's cope and miter from the sacristy and helps him or her with them. The cope is heavy and can be difficult to put on in a hurry without help. The server then retrieves the crook from the altar and gives it to the bishop so that he or she has it for the final blessing.

These are the traditional positions but that does not mean that every parish must divide duties in this way. In smaller parishes, the server and crucifer positions are often combined, and in other parishes torchbearers are assigned only for special occasions, if at all. To see step-by-step procedures and possible cues from the acolyte's point of view, see the Parish Acolyte's Guide.

Chapter 5
Understanding the Eucharistic Service:
An Overview Including Acolyte Involvement

Understanding the parts of the service and how they fit together prepares you, as the acolyte leader, to plan how the acolytes can best assist the clergy with worship. It also helps you communicate more easily with the clergy and avoid misunderstanding. Included in this chapter you will find a brief summary of the parts of the Episcopal eucharistic service, including possible acolyte involvement. If the parish has one or more deacons, or a strong corps of lay ministers, some of the duties listed below may be assigned to them. In any case, the acolyte's goal must always be to assist the priest to provide a smooth flowing, prayerful worship service.

To get the most out of this chapter, open your prayer book and page through it from beginning to end. Make a list of the most commonly used services in your parish and then read the rubrics (the italicized instructions) for those services.

Rite One and Two services can most simply be broken into four parts, the Entrance Rite, the Liturgy of the Word, the Great Thanksgiving, and the Dismissal. The summary description below will give you an understanding of the basics that the priest you work with must consider. Changes and additions are necessary for special services, of course, but by understanding what is normal, we have a better understanding of what is special.

Before the Service

Traditionally, services begin with a time of meditation, usually the fifteen minutes before the entrance or procession. To begin the time of meditation, the crucifer or server lights the eucharistic candles and/or office lights in the sanctuary.

The Entrance Rite

This is the first part of the service and includes the formal entrance of the priest and service team, hymns, psalms, and prayers of preparation including the collect for purity and a collect specific to the day in the church calendar. The goal is to gather and prepare the people for prayer.

The formal entrance may be in the form of a procession, with music, starting from the back of the church (through and of the people) and includes acolytes, the choir, assistant or lay ministers, and the priest or priests. Festival processions can include even more people and may be vastly more elaborate (see Chapter 6 on processions). On the other hand, the entrance may be simple and include only an acolyte and priest entering from the sacristy. The acolytes help set the tone of celebration or solemn dignity appropriate to the service with their vestments, posture, and attitude.

The Liturgy of the Word

The Liturgy of the Word is the second part of the service and includes the lessons and psalms, the gospel, the homily or sermon, the Nicene Creed, the prayers of the people, the confession and absolution, and the peace. During this part of the service, the people hear God's word proclaimed, have it interpreted in the homily, affirm their belief through the creed, have an opportunity to lift up their concerns in prayer, and finally prepare themselves to approach God's presence through confession and absolution and reconciliation or peace with each other.

The lessons and psalm are most often read by lay people. In a small service or when the assigned lector hasn't arrived, an acolyte can be asked to read the lessons and lead the psalms. And while only a priest or deacon traditionally reads the gospel for a eucharistic service, an acolyte or other lay person may read it for Morning Prayer. For more formal services, acolytes often provide a gospel procession with torches and the gospel book. The torches, while no longer needed as extra lighting, help separate and highlight the gospel reading. Whether the reading takes place at the pulpit or in the center of the church, having an acolyte hold the gospel book emphasizes that the words are being "proclaimed" and are not the words of the speaker.

Having heard the word, had it explained, affirmed our belief, we next bring our concerns to God in the prayers of the people. These may be lead by a priest, a deacon, or by a lay person appointed by the priest. A senior acolyte can lead the prayers, but as it takes some practice to comfortably lead prayers, they are not often asked to do so.

Acolytes should participate fully in the peace, but will also find that it is a convenient moment for the priest to ask for help with "midcourse corrections." Acolytes may be asked to slip out quietly to the sacristy for a forgotten piece of linen or equipment, take a message to the Sunday school, or ask an extra lay minister to vest and assist with Communion. These and other simple tasks can be taken care of quietly and without disrupting the service during the announcements that generally follow the peace.

The Holy Communion

This segment of the service has several distinct parts and consists of the Offertory, the Great Thanksgiving, the Breaking of the Bread (the fraction), the administration of Communion, and the postcommunion prayer.

The Offertory includes the bread, wine, and alms as the gifts of the people. In early centuries of the church, each person brought bread and wine as well as other offerings in kind and left them at the church door. The amount of bread and wine needed was used for Communion and any extra was used to feed the clergy and the poor. Money is more convenient to carry than a loaf of bread but is nonetheless the fruits of our labor, a portion of which we offer to God. The acolyte gives the collection plates to the ushers and accepts the bread, water, and wine offering and takes them to the credence table.

The acolyte takes first the bread and then the wine and water to the priest at the altar to be prepared for the Eucharist. If incense is used (another offering), the priest will cense the altar and gifts. After that, either the deacon or the thurifer may cense (a form of cleansing) the priest, lay or assisting ministers, and the congregation. Next, the acolyte assists the priest with the ceremonial hand washing (the lavabo) and then goes back to accept the alms basin and/or collection plates and gives them to the priest to be presented.

Once the table and the offerings have been prepared, the service continues with the Great Thanksgiving. Many parishes use the Sanctus bells during this portion of the service. One appropriate place to use the bells is during the acclamation in the Sanctus (the words "Holy, Holy, Holy" are an acclamation). When music is not used, the acolyte rings the Sanctus bells three times, once at each "Holy." In parishes in which music is used, the Sanctus bells are sometimes rung before the music begins. After the responses, the acolytes and congregation may kneel (especially in Rite One). In the Episcopal Church, either standing or kneeling is an option and both show respect. Acolytes provide an example here, especially for newcomers. When the acolytes and assisting ministers kneel or stand, the congregation tends to do the same. It is important that acolytes know what is customary for the congregation.

The Eucharistic Prayer tells the story of the last supper and remembers the sacrifice and resurrection that is the basis of our Communion. The Sanctus bells are used in many parishes to remind us of the presence of the Holy Spirit in Communion and to reverence the moments at which the priest elevates the bread and wine and repeats Jesus' words, "Do this for the remembrance of me." On a practical front, the human mind tends to wander and the bells recall our minds sharply to focus at important points in the prayers. The service continues with the Lord's Prayer followed by the actual breaking of the bread referred to as the fraction.

After the fraction, the priest prepares the consecrated bread and wine to feed the congregation. If actual loaves of bread are used, it has to be broken at this point and placed on patens or plates. The paten may be too small to safely hold the bread, and larger plates or trays might be needed. Depending on the size of the congregation, the amount of wine needed, and the number of priests and assisting ministers, the wine may have been consecrated in a single chalice, in two chalices, or in a cruet or flagon. If extra chalices and plates are needed, a deacon, assisting priest, or acolyte brings them quietly to the altar from the credence table at this point. The priest then invites the congregation to Communion. The priests receive Communion themselves and communicate the deacon and lay ministers. As a matter of practicality, they often give Communion to the altar team, organist, and choir before the congregation comes forward for Communion.

After the congregation has received Communion, any remaining consecrated bread or wine has to be consumed and the vessels cleaned. The ablutions can be done either directly after Communion, or the vessels may be covered and placed on the credence table or moved to the sacristy by the deacon, lay ministers, or priests to be dealt with after the service. When the ablutions are done directly after Communion, the acolyte usually brings the cruet of water and pours into the chalice at the priest's signal, returns the cruet to the credence table, and waits by the altar to be given extra chalices or other items that need to be removed to the credence table. For larger services, this may take several trips. If there are several priests or a deacon, they may help carry items to the credence table in the interest of time and preparing for the postcommunion prayer.

Before kneeling for the postcommunion prayer, the acolyte checks the credence table to see that all stoppers and lids have been replaced, that the table is relatively tidy, and that nothing is so close to the edge that it might fall or be bumped by passing service team members. If the vessels are to be cleaned later, chalices and patens should be covered.

The Dismissal

The last part of the service includes the blessing of the people, a formal exit procession, and a dismissal.

If a bishop is present, he or she blesses the people. If a bishop is not present, the priest may offer a blessing. This is often followed by a recessional hymn that serves to get the acolytes, choir, lay ministers, and priest to the back of the church or to the sacristy. At this point, an acolyte extinguishes the eucharistic and service candles. This is followed by a formal dismissal given by either a deacon or priest. When there is neither a formal exit procession nor a closing hymn, the acolyte, lay ministers, and priest may simply exit to the sacristy or go directly to the back of the church. Either way, the priest usually allows a few moments of silent prayer, during which the acolyte extinguishes the altar candles, before dismissing the congregation.

The Baptismal Service

The service of Holy Baptism with a Eucharist contains the same elements as the service outlined above. A special entrance rite and the beginning of the Liturgy of the Word begin on page 299 of the Book of Common Prayer. After the baptism, the service reverts to the Rite One or Rite Two service. The acolyte support needs to be adjusted, however.

If the baptismal font is in the back of the church or significantly away from the altar, acolytes may be asked to lead a procession with torches and processional cross, baptismal candidates, families, sponsors, server, and priest to and from the font. This adds a ceremonial touch and moves the participants quickly and in an orderly manner. At the font, the server often holds the prayer book for the priest while his or her hands are occupied. Depending on the location of the font, the acolyte may be asked to bring the water to be blessed from the sacristy. Acolytes may be asked to light the baptismal candle from the Paschal candle and hand it to the priest or present it, when told, to the baptized or their sponsor. Acolytes often distribute the baptismal certificates to family members either during the Baptism or immediately after the service dismissal.

After the actual Baptism, acolytes are usually the ones who clear away extra tables or items of equipment before the service continues with either the Prayers of the People or the Offertory. For extra insight on the baptismal service, read the instructions on page 298 and 312 of the Book of Common Prayer.

Other Services and Duties

Special services such as those in Holy Week, festival services, and weddings and funerals all contain some of the same structure as the Rite One and Rite Two services. To prepare for those services, review the rubrics for the particular service in the Book of Common Prayer before discussing it with your parish priest. See Chapter 7 on planning and managing special services. An acolyte's duties can include almost anything that assists the priest to do his or her job faster or better, particularly when he or she has large numbers of communicants to serve. In 1999 a senior acolyte in a parish in Pennsylvania was assigned to serve a visiting bishop from India. The acolyte met him at the door, showed him the sacristy, hung up his vestments, and then asked if there was anything else she could do for him. The bishop had a sense of humor and immediately replied, "Yes, how about giving the sermon for me?" She grinned and replied, "No problem. May I use your notes?" He laughed and said, "You are a good servant!" Of course she didn't give the sermon, but she did escort him to the pulpit and after the service, helped him put on his shoes. In India, shoes are not worn in sanctuaries, and the bishop had removed his for the service. As he was having trouble bending over to put them back on and needed to rush off to meet with parishioners, the acolyte dropped to her knees and helped. Performing that simple task allowed the bishop to get on with serving others in the parish.

Acolytes are servants of God and his Church.

Chapter 6
Planning and Managing Processions

Processions provide a touch of ceremony, mark the formal beginning and end of services, and move both people and the attention of the congregation from one point to another. Processions also set the tone for the congregation and signal what will follow in a particular service. For example, the silent, solemn procession often used in Lent encourages sober reflection, whereas a festival procession at Easter draws us into the celebration. With or without conscious explanation, we subconsciously respond to the tone and symbolism of the procession.

In parishes that have a traditional verger, he or she normally plans and leads processions. In many parishes, however, the acolyte leader assists the deacon or priest with this job.

Planning a procession begins with understanding the purpose of the procession and how it fits into the service. It is also important to know at the outset who needs to be included and the order of precedence. All of which has to be balanced with practical common sense.

Formal Versus Informal Processions

The choice between a formal or informal procession depends greatly on the type of service, the occasion, and the traditions or personality of the parish. An informal entry procession, including only an acolyte, lay minister, and priest that serves to get them from the sacristy to the altar, is simple, elegant, and looks natural. But it still has its rules and practical considerations. For example, the celebrating priest always enters last and ends up at the center behind the altar, in position to start the service. The group reverences the altar together and the acolyte and lay minister go directly to their seats. This simple, natural (if all goes well), almost solemn entry alerts the congregation to stand and begin the service.

Informal, however, does not mean sloppy. As with other elements of the service, an informal procession depends on everyone knowing where they're going, moving smoothly and quietly without hurrying, and therefore keeping the attention of the congregation focused on worship rather than on mistakes made by service participants.

A formal entry procession, on the other hand, involves more people, more symbolism, and usually includes music. It sets a different tone or mood for worship while moving the priest, ministers, and others directly involved in the service into the sanctuary. A formal entry procession usually begins at the back of the church, so that the priest and service assistants arrive from among the people. In cathedrals or other large churches, a procession may even begin from a side door or from more than one location and move through and around the area occupied by the congregation as a way to draw the congregation more fully into the service. It can include a processional cross, torchbearers, choir (optional), lay ministers, server, deacon, assisting priests, and the celebrating priest. Again there are rules (see below).

Types of Processions

There are basically three types of processions. An entry procession (formal or informal) is actually part of the Entrance Rite that begins the eucharistic service. An exit or retiring procession moves the service participants out of the sanctuary quickly and signals the end of the service. During the service, positioning processions highlight an activity or move the action and the congregation's attention from the altar to another part of the church.

Who and What to Include

On most occasions and for most services, processions include only those people who actually have a part to play in leading or supporting the service. Whether or not participants such as the lectors and the choir process often depends on where they sit during the service. For example, if the choir occupies a gallery at the back of the church, it may not be practical to process them. However, depending on the tradition of the parish, they may be processed anyway.

The exceptions (there are always exceptions) include Palm Sunday when many parishes include the entire congregation in what is, in effect, a reenactment of Christ's entry into Jerusalem. Another exception is funeral services. Family members and pallbearers usually sit with the congregation, but depending on parish tradition, may be part of the procession.

Basic Rules for Organizing a Procession

Like all rules, these are guidelines that generally have a practical basis.

The goal of a procession planner is to estimate the time a procession will take, the number of participants in the procession, and the pace so as to have the last person, the celebrating priest, arrive at his or her place by the middle of the last verse of the processional hymn. Long processions should be cued and paced so that no one has to stand and wait in the aisle (no traffic jams). For festival or extremely long processions, this may mean stationing someone (yourself or a senior acolyte) at the door of the sanctuary to slow down the rate at which people move into the aisle and join the procession.

If the parish has a verger, he or she will normally process first. Otherwise, either the thurifer or the crucifer and torchbearers come first in processions. For practical reasons, the thurifer often processes first, leaving a wide gap (as much as half the length of the processional route) between him or herself and the rest of the procession.

The celebrating priest usually comes last in the procession. If a visiting bishop (he or she is also a priest) is present, he or she is automatically considered to be the celebrant and processes last with his or her chaplain or server directly in front. When several bishops are present, the diocesan bishop has precedence. He or she processes last (whether or not he or she is acting as the celebrant) and other bishops, whether or not formally involved in the service, may be placed further forward in the procession.

The banner represents the congregation or a visiting dignitary and is therefore positioned directly in front of whatever it represents. If members of the congregation, such as on Palm Sunday or Confirmation, are included in the procession, they follow the banner. Otherwise, it can be placed in front of the choir or lectors. If neither the choir nor other members of the congregation are included, consider not using the parish banner. Parishes sometimes use a special event banner, which may be, but are not often, used without members of the congregation in the procession.

In special processions, the U.S. flag and the Episcopal Church flag may be processed, usually directly in front of the banner. The order of procession goes from Christ (represented by the processional cross and torches), the United States and the Episcopal Church, with their flags side by side (the U.S. flag is always on the right-hand side), followed by the congregation and its banner.

Two additional torchbearers may be assigned to light the way for visiting dignitaries such as the presiding or a senior bishop. In cathedrals, four torchbearers are sometimes assigned, two in front of the dignitary and two behind, to light the way and to allow the people to see the dignitary clearly. The arrangement of four torches is sometimes referred to as the Canterbury Configuration or Canterbury Square and may also be used for special gospel processions.

If two sets of crucifers and torchbearers are used, the second set is positioned directly in front of the clergy. For long or complex processions, this is a natural point for a pause to adjust the pace and allow time to clear any delays that may have left people standing in the aisle.

Finally, the order of procession (between the crucifer and the celebrating priest) is often based on where participants are to be seated, and seating is usually based on precedence and/or the participant's part in the service. Particularly in small sanctuaries or for large services, arranging a smooth procession is a balance of social or historical precedence and common sense.

A procession doesn't end until everyone is standing in front of the right chair. Seating cards are helpful in preventing last minute confusion. See Chapter 7, Planning and Managing Special Services, for more on seating cards.

Order of Procession

A formal entry procession usually proceeds in this order:

Crucifer
Torchbearers (behind or beside the crucifer)
Choir (optional)
Lectors (only if they sit with the service team)
Lay ministers
Server
Assisting priest(s)
Deacon of the Mass
Celebrating Priest

A celebration procession adds a few more participants:

Crucifer
Two torchbearers (beside or behind the crucifer)
Banner bearer
Members of the congregation
Choir
Lectors (only if they sit with the service team)
Lay ministers
Server
Assisting priest(s)
Deacon
Celebrating Priest

For a festival procession, it is often necessary to include short pauses between groups to help smooth the pace and keep the procession from backing up in the aisles. Optional positions and appropriate points for pauses are shown in the following festival procession order:

Boat bearer
Thurifer
Pause—

Lead crucifer
Two torchbearers (beside or behind the crucifer)
*Book bearer
Banner bearer
Junior choir
Choir
Lectors
Pause—
Clergy crucifer
Clergy torchbearers
Lay ministers
Assisting priests
Visiting priest(s)
Deacon
Server
Rector
Bishop's chaplain or server
Bishop

*If the deacon or a member of the clergy carries the book instead of an acolyte, he or she takes their normal place in procession.

For planning purposes, review what positions are needed for a special, celebration, or festival service, and then eliminate those not needed. Begin with the verger (if you have one), the thurifer or crucifer and end with the celebrating priest. Organize those in the middle according to precedence and the seating available. Note that the server, who normally processes in front of the assisting priest(s), is usually placed in front of the rector in a festival service (depending on seating) so as not to be separated from him or her by two groups.

Special Positioning Processions

Processions used within the framework of a service for positioning, such as the gospel procession, usually include only the crucifer and/or the two torchbearers and the person or people being moved. The processional cross may or may not be used. In many parishes, the crucifer acts as the book bearer, carrying and holding the gospel book for the deacon or priest to read. If a separate book bearer has been assigned, he or she does this. In either case, the two torchbearers provide extra illumination and add a touch of ceremony.

Other positioning processions are organized based on the needs of the service. For example, the crucifer and torchbearers may lead the families involved in Baptism to the font and back to their seats. During a funeral, the crucifer and torchbearers may lead family members to the columbarium (if it is in the church) for the committal. Such processions save time by moving people efficiently and quickly with no break in the service.

Processional Routes

The best processional routes are the simplest—partly because the procession itself takes time and tends to be ornate enough without convoluted routes. For example, an entry procession generally moves straight up the center aisle and (depending on the layout of the church) splits at the altar rail, or moves together around the rail taking the most direct route to their seats. As always, there are exceptions. For example, on Palm Sunday in many parishes, the procession begins outside the church and may circle the interior, or trace a figure eight if the side aisles are wide enough.

Retiring or Exit Processions

A retiring or exit procession, with or without music, moves the service participants and the priest out of the sanctuary and signals a formal close to the service. If practical, the same people who processed also recess in the same order. An example of when it may not be practical includes Confirmation. Candidates may be included in a procession fairly smoothly, but stopping the exit while they file out of their pews to join in takes time and adds nothing to the formal close. The order may also be changed for other practical reasons. For example, when a visiting bishop or other dignitary is present and his or her time with the congregation is short, the processional order behind the crucifer is occasionally reversed so that the bishop(s) and priests exit first.

One Last Thing

To increase your chances of success in moving a large number of people smoothly into or out of a service, first, keep it simple. Second, make sure everyone involved knows where they fit in the procession. Finally, (as insurance) if your parish doesn't have a verger, provide the senior acolyte with an index card with the order of procession to tuck in a pocket and teach him or her how to unobtrusively direct traffic if needed.

Chapter 7
Planning and Managing Special Services

Arranging acolyte support for special, celebration, or festival services takes time, effort, and coordination. Success often lies in understanding the details and making sure that everyone else does too. In larger parishes, the verger, deacon, or perhaps an assisting priest (working with the rector) generally plans and coordinates festival services. In smaller parishes the acolyte leader often does this job. Either way, acolytes cannot operate in a vacuum. Making sure that acolytes, ushers, the choir director, and anyone else involved in the service knows what to expect is key to success.

Planning

Planning begins with understanding what the priest envisions. A simple way to do this is to review the service with the priest, section by section, using the prayer book. Ask specifically about additions or changes such as congregational candlelight, foot washing, or distribution of palms, and how these will be incorporated in the service. Having a rough floor plan of your church on hand during this discussion saves time and helps both priest and planner visualize the service and clarify the details. A sample floor plan that can be used as a basis to create your own is included at the end of this chapter.

Once you clearly understand the priest's vision of the service, you can discuss which specific jobs the acolytes will handle and which will be handled by the deacon, ushers, verger, and/or other members of the service team. Record these on a sheet of paper or on a copy of your festival check sheet on page 42. This is also the point in planning to suggest changes in the acolyte support and/or offer additional help. For example, extra chairs may need to be placed or extra equipment retrieved from storage.

Once you know what changes or additional elements will be included, it's important to agree on how these will be incorporated into the service. In short, you need to set cues. Using a cue worksheet, like the one provided on page 43, ensures that you have a clear understanding of when and how each job needs to be done.

The cues chosen need to be simple and based on obvious elements in the service such as the peace, the announcements, or the beginning of a particular hymn. If a cue is based on the actions of an individual, such as the crucifer picking up the gospel book, then the action needs to be obvious and highly visible. It is best to avoid cues that depend on a member of the service team nodding, pointing, or catching the eye of an acolyte, as that person may forget or be distracted.

While planning cues, pay particular attention to transitions in the service. The ideal is for the transitions to be smooth and unnoticed by the congregation. Extra tasks can often be fitted neatly into something that is already happening. If not, the music director can often cover a minute or two with an extra hymn or a few seconds of "walking music." For example, the bishop's chair can be left in front of the altar after the actual Confirmation and moved to make way for Communion during the peace or the offertory. On the other hand, moving the crucifer, torchbearers, and several families back to their pews after a multiple Baptism may need to be covered with a hymn or just a minute or two of organ music.

For complex festival services, it is helpful for the assigned senior acolyte and/or crucifer to help refine the cues that they will be using, during a walk-through of the service.

Next, physically check and make a list of the extra equipment that will be needed (for example, thurible, extra chairs, a second set of torches). Include these on the check sheet and note on the floor plan where they need to be placed. Ask if seat cards will be needed.

The opportunities for mishaps and embarrassing moments abound in festival and special services, especially when visiting clergy and extra service participants may not have an opportunity to attend the rehearsal. A simple seating chart and seat cards are one way to ensure that a stately procession doesn't end in a game of musical chairs. For a simple seating chart, make a copy of your church layout plan, write in the names under each chair, and post it in the vesting area so that participants can double-check before the procession. For simple seating cards, print the titles of participants on index paper and cut cards approximately three inches high by eight inches wide. Print position titles (or use a felt tip marker) large enough to be read from a distance. Place the cards on the floor under the edge of each chair and they will be easily visible to service participants but not visible at all to the congregation. Use the cards during rehearsal to ensure that visiting clergy or others who could not attend haven't been forgotten in seating arrangements.

Before you complete your service plan, consider who will be involved in supporting the service besides the priest, lay ministers, and acolytes. The necessary coordination for a special service may or may not be part of your job, but ensuring that all the service team members know what to expect is good insurance. For example, making sure the ushers know when to turn off the main lights for a candlelight service ensures that acolytes aren't left stumbling in the dark at an inappropriate moment. Sharing your organized checklist and cue sheet with other service team members also gives them the opportunity to clear up misperceptions and solve potential problems before they occur.

Once your plan is complete, it is helpful to go back to the priest and show him or her your checklist, cue sheet, and floor plan. This provides an opportunity for the priest to review the service and planned support and make any changes or adjustments he or she may have thought of in the meantime.

If the service is a large or unusual one, such as the Christmas Midnight Mass or a Confirmation, a short walk-through rehearsal with the acolytes ensures that everyone is comfortable with what will be expected. A rehearsal need not last more than twenty to thirty minutes and can be scheduled after a regular Sunday service for convenience. Besides giving new acolytes a chance to see and practice their part in the service, a rehearsal also gives the priest another opportunity to change or add additional elements to the service and to review the assigned seating and make adjustments if needed.

The walk-through rehearsal is also the time to refine the equipment list and assign acolytes to help place the equipment and seating cards before the service. The rehearsal usually ends with a reminder of the time acolytes and other participants are expected to arrive before the actual service.

Managing the Service Preparation

Detailed planning and coordinating will prevent most problems. However, someone still has to come in early before the service, check all the details, answer the questions, and solve last-minute problems. In short, someone needs to manage the service preparation.

When there is no verger, this job is often shared by the priest and acolyte leader. Preparing a clean copy of the checklist and floor plan a few days before the service gives you an opportunity to review and make sure that details aren't being overlooked, that is, that equipment has been repaired or delivered as needed, vestments have been cleaned, and that reminder postcards have been sent to the acolytes (if the rehearsal took place two or more weeks before the service, this is a good idea).

Arriving early the day of the service with checklist, floor plan, and cue sheet in hand (or on a clip board), you should be able to quickly and easily check that equipment and seat cards are in place, that acolytes have arrived and are vested, and that everybody knows their cues. The crucifer can use the cue sheet to help organize and check the procession. The crucifer should also check the length of the processional hymn and adjust the procession start cue if the hymn is a short one. Offer a copy of the cue sheet and floor plan to your priest to help him or her review the service with visiting clergy. Post another copy of the floor plan with clearly marked seating in the procession assembly area so that acolytes as well as visitors can double-check assigned seating or processional order before the service.

Last, as the processional begins, it may be helpful to post someone at the sanctu-ary door, or wherever the procession begins, to help set and maintain the distance between elements. Longer processions can bunch up and stop altogether if partic-ipants join the procession too quickly.

Once you have a floor plan, a checklist, and a cue sheet for each of the usual special services in your parish, for example, Christmas, Confirmations, weddings, funerals, and Holy Week, the planning comes down to changes from the norm. However, never forget that success is in the details, and that detailed planning, every time, supports success.

Sample Church Layout

T=Torchbearer
LC=Lead Crucifer
CC=Clergy Crucifer
TH=Thurible
S=Server
LEM=Lay Eucharistic Minister

Having a basic floor plan helps you see the whole space when planning service support. It also simplifies discussions with the priest, and instructions for the acolytes. Using paper, pencil, and ruler (or a word processing program as was used here), make a simple floor plan of your own church to keep on hand.

```
 T ⊃     _____         ⊂ TH
 T ⊃     _____              Door
 T ⊃     _____Choir_____
 T ⊃     _____              O
 CC ⊃   ⊕ S   LEM    Visiting    Priest    Visiting   LC ⊕         R
                      Priest               Priest                  G
                                                       Prayer      A
                                                       Desk/LEM    N
    _____                                            ⊂
  Credence
   Table
              I                               I                    Door
              I        I    Altar     I       I
              I        I_____ I       I
              I                               I
              I---Rail--------   -----Rail--------I

      Π Pulpit                              Lectern
    ⊗ Banner stand                            II

    ○Banner bearer_____        _____
 S  _____         _____       S
 i  _____         _____       i
 d  _____         _____       d
 e  _____         _____       e
    _____         _____
 A  _____         _____   A   A
 i  _____         _____       i
 s  _____         _____       s
 l  _____         _____       l
 e  _____         _____       e
    _____         _____
    _____         _____
    _____         _____
    _____         _____
    _____         _____

    ⊕ Baptismal                      Banner stand
    font                                ⊗

                      door _____
```

Checklist for Festival Services

Type of Service _____ Begins at _____ o'clock.
(i.e., Christmas, Easter, Confirmation)

1. Scheduling

Position	Names	Confirmed?
Thurifer	_____	_____
Lead crucifer	_____	_____
Torchbearer	_____	_____
Torchbearer	_____	_____
Boat bearer	_____	_____
Banner bearer	_____	_____
Clergy crucifer	_____	_____
Torchbearer	_____	_____
Torchbearer	_____	_____
Book bearer	_____	_____
Server	_____	_____
Senior acolyte	_____	_____

2. Service cues determined with priest? Yes/No. Cue sheet attached.

3. Altar seating agreed? (Plan attached). Seating cards? Yes/No.

4. Vestments chosen? _____.

5. Extra equipment needed _____, _____, _____.

6. Who positions extra equipment? _____ When? _____.

7. Extra jobs before the service _____, _____
(i.e., add extra chairs. Continue on back of sheet if necessary.)

8. Check processional hymn against the length of the procession _____ .

9. Who needs to know processional or service cues? _____,
_____, _____, _____.

10. Processional assembly area and route? _____.

11. Acolyte rehearsal date/time? _____.

12. Reminder notices or phone calls? Yes/No. Arrival time for vesting and final
instructions? _____.

Cue Worksheet

Type of Service _____ Begins at _____ o'clock.
(i.e., Baptism, Christmas, Easter, Confirmation?)

Before the Service (i.e. light Advent wreath) _____
_____

Order of Procession (Delete any not needed or add others)

Order	Participants	Names
	Thurifer	_____
	Lead crucifer	_____
	Torchbearers	_____ , _____
	Boat bearer	_____
	Banner bearer	_____
	Congregation members	_____
	Choir	_____
	Clergy crucifer	_____
	Torchbearers	_____ , _____
	Book	_____
	Lay ministers	_____ , _____
	Visiting clergy	_____ , _____
	Server	_____
	Assisting parish	_____ , _____
	clergy	_____
	Rector	_____
	Bishop's server	_____
	Bishop	_____

Cue to begin procession: _____

Cue and route for internal procession (i.e., to baptismal font) _____

route _____

Cue for gospel procession _____

Extra equipment or furniture needed (i.e. Bishop's chair)

_____

Cue to position? _____, Cue to remove? _____

Other extra duties

Server: _____ Cue _____

Crucifer: _____ Cue _____

Torchbearers: _____ Cue _____

Thurifer: _____ Cue _____

Banner bearer: _____ Cue _____

Boat bearer: _____ Cue _____

Book bearer: _____ Cue _____

Cue to begin exit procession:

_____

Change of order for exit procession:

_____

Notes:

Chapter 8
Managing the Program: Recruiting, Training, and Rewarding

Supervising acolytes takes only an hour or two each Sunday morning. Managing the program takes a great deal more. Three of the most challenging aspects of managing any ministry are recruiting people to do the job, training them, and recognizing or rewarding them for their efforts.

Of course there is more to managing any group of volunteers, but these particular elements are foundations. Encouraging and trusting acolytes is just as important and often makes the difference between an acolyte who stays one year (or less) and an acolyte who grows into the ministry over a number of years.

Recruiting

Recruiting is a recurring task from year to year. In parishes where a good many of the acolytes are young people, high school graduation can create significant gaps in the ranks of servers. Other acolytes occasionally move on to other ministries. Fortunately, the task of recruiting is made easier by the limited audience you need to reach.

One easy approach is to decide on a training day for new acolytes and then announce that fact repeatedly. Most people need to see an announcement several times before they respond. The announcement also needs to be made far enough in advance (at least a month) to give possible candidates time to fit the training into busy calendars.

A simple way to get the word out is to include an announcement in the monthly parish newsletter or the weekly service bulletins for at least two to four weeks before the scheduled training session. Include eye-catching graphics. The announcement should be short and simple but include when, where, who is invited, how long the session will last, and a phone number for more information. For example:

A new acolyte training session is scheduled for Sunday, August 15, after the 10:15 A.M. service in the church. Anyone considering the ministry of acolytes is invited to attend. The session will last one hour. For more information, call (name), acolyte leader, at 555-2525."

Using two, three, or even four different methods to announce training ensures that as many people as possible either see the announcement or hear about it from friends. Word of mouth is an effective additional, but not primary, tool. Ask your priest to help spread the word with announcements during the services and by discussing the ministry with parishioners after the services and during the week. Also ask current acolytes to spread the word and discuss their service with friends in the parish.

On the other hand, some people (particularly those who are shy or retiring) need a more personal approach. Ask your priest, the Confirmation class leader, and Sunday school teachers (adult class too) if they can recommend anyone you should approach with a personal invitation. An invitation letter (on disk that you can personalize, print, and mail quickly) is an effective recruiting tool that is personal, affirming, and hard to resist.

It is important to understand, however, that recruiting methods that work in one parish may not work in another. Try different approaches and if one approach doesn't work or gets stale, try another. For example, explore ways to educate the parish about the ministry. Consider offering a presentation for groups, such as the youth group or bible study class, and at parish gatherings. You can set up a display during coffee hour or write an article for your parish newsletter or magazine. Contact acolyte leaders in other parishes, explore their methods, and share ideas.

Training

Acolyte training is as personal as the acolyte leader and as individual as the parish concerned. Any training method will have to be adapted to meet the needs of the parish, the priest, and the leader. A few guidelines however, apply universally when it comes to training people of any age, for any skill.

- First, the most effective training sessions last an hour or less. If more time is necessary, a five to ten minute break each hour allows everyone to stretch, visit the bathroom, take a mental break, and return fresh and focused on the subject.
- Take-home material, in this case an acolyte manual, allows students to review the training before actually serving, and increases their confidence with specific tasks and their own ability to serve. The Parish Acolyte's Guide, a companion to this book, explains acolyte duties step-by-step and includes space to write in details and cues specific to your parish.
- The best way to learn a skill is hands-on practice. After a brief overview of general rules and expectations, consider dividing new acolytes into small groups under the supervision of senior, more experienced acolytes who can walk them through each task, make minor corrections, share the tricks they've learned, and allow new acolytes to practice until they are comfortable.
- The best trainers are often the people who are most experienced with the

same duties. More experienced (no matter what age) acolytes have experience with balancing torches and processional crosses, timing and pacing, and the little tricks that make serving easier. Asking them to act as trainers or mentors (with a checklist of subjects you particularly want covered) ensures that each new acolyte gets the individual attention he or she may need to be comfortable in his or her duties. Just as importantly, it also encourages leadership and helps senior acolytes polish their own skills. A sample trainer's checklist is provided at the end of this chapter.

Rewards, Recognition, and Incentives

According to Webster's Dictionary, a reward is "something given in return for something done." For most acolytes, the service is its own reward. However, there's no getting around the incentive effect of rewards, especially for younger acolytes and those considering the ministry.

Rewards can take many shapes. Some parishes organize an annual group trip to an amusement park as thanks for acolyte service. Some parishes give each acolyte a small gift such as a cross or lapel pin each year. Other parishes recognize acolytes during a particular service each year, calling their names, and asking them to stand and be recognized and thanked by the congregation. This last combines both recognition and reward. Another parish has a special acolyte's service one Sunday a year for which all acolytes vest and process. New acolytes are vested and blessed during the announcements.

Recognizing an acolyte for one, three, or five years of service, whether he or she is leaving the parish or not, is another option that has real value and is connected to a specific contribution to the parish. Presenting a simple thank-you gift during the announcements in a Sunday service allows the entire congregation to share in the acknowledgment and thanks. There is no need to wait until an acolyte completes their service or leaves the parish. Having special rewards for years of service is also a way to include adult acolytes who remain with the parish and provide faithful service over a number of years.

"Award" on the other hand, is defined in that same dictionary as "to give a prize." The expectation with an award program is that individuals will be recognized as being better than their peers at something in particular.

An award such as one for the "most hours of service" leaves open the discussion that some acolytes may have been scheduled more or less often than others, and therefore had more opportunities. An award based on categories such as "most helpful" leave the door open to accusations of favoritism.

While an award program can be an incentive, it may also encourage competition and cause hard feelings, neither of which is conducive to the team spirit an acolyte program needs.

Sample Recruiting Letter

Church Letterhead or Notepaper

                                                    Date _____

Dear _____,

Father _____ and I invite you to become an acolyte.

There will be a training session for all acolytes on Sunday, March 17, after the family service. The session will last approximately one hour. Why not come to that, get an idea of what acolytes are all about, and then decide for yourself?

If you are interested, but can't make this training session, please let me know and we can arrange an alternate training time. You can reach me at 555-2525.

I hope to see you on March 17.

Yours in Service,

(signed)
Acolyte Leader

Sample Trainer or Mentor's Checklist

Torchbearer Trainer's Notes:

___ 1. Help the new acolytes fit vestments.

___ 2. Explain balance points.
  *One hand at the bridge of the nose, other hand at waist.
  *Keep torch upright.

___ 3. Height
  *Put the flame just under the cross bar.
  *Check that torches are level between partners (have them face each other
   before processing and adjust).

___ 4. Practice going up and down stairs without leaning.

___ 5. Pace
  *Practice even pace with partners.
  *Almost shoulder to shoulder.
  *Practice mirror movements.

___ 6. Cues for a regular Sunday (walk-through the service)
  *Procession cue = follow crucifer
  *Gospel cue = beginning of the hymn
  *Exit = beginning of the last hymn and then watch crucifer

___ 7. Routes for special services—especially Baptisms

___ 8. If you have time
  *Special jobs for torches, for example, lighting hand candles
  *Canterbury Square

___ 9. Refer them to the Acolyte Manual for questions and point out
   the Phone Roster.

___ 10.. Welcome them to the program.

New torchbearer: _____

Trainer: _____

THANK YOU! Please return this sheet to me after training.

Chapter 9
Administrative Chores Made Easy

Administrative tasks such as scheduling, budgeting, reports and other necessary paperwork can turn a fun volunteer activity into a part-time job. However, they don't have to. Building your own forms, formats, and administrative tools from the information and samples provided in this chapter can help cut operating chores down to size.

Scheduling

In some parishes, the acolyte leader alone schedules acolytes. In other parishes, the secretary or clerk of the parish schedules acolytes as well as ushers, lay ministers, nursery helpers, and other service participants. Even in the latter case, individual leaders or chair people usually schedule for special services. Either way, the acolyte leader must still provide the information needed to do the job, starting with a comprehensive, up-to-date acolyte roster that includes names, addresses, phone numbers, and the positions each acolyte has been trained for and can be scheduled against.

For parishes with small acolyte programs, scheduling can usually be handled using a simple rotation. For example, starting from the most senior acolyte to the least (or the other way round), assign each a number from one to ten (or however many you have), and then keep track by entering the number and the date last served in a separate column on a copy of the acolyte roster. If 1 to 4 served last month, then schedule 5 through 8 this month, and then 9, 10, 1, and 2 the month following. If you separate torchbearers, crucifers, and servers, you can use the same rotation within categories. When adding sisters and brothers who need to serve at the same service, or torchbearers of the same general height whom you may want to schedule together, simply number them, for example, as 4a and b rather than by seniority. This may mean restarting the numbering every year to keep it from getting overly complicated. As an alternative, the numbering can be started with 10, 20, 30, and so forth. New acolytes added to the schedule would be given numbers in between. For example, if an acolyte whose schedule number was 20 encouraged his brother to join, the brother's schedule number could be 21. If their mom then joined, her number could be 22.

In the same vein, you can assign acolytes into teams of torchbearers, crucifer, and server and then assign the teams in rotation.

Assigning acolytes at random is also a possibility, but depending on the number of acolytes to be scheduled, it can be difficult after a time to avoid the appearance of favoring some acolytes or scheduling others less than their peers.

After scheduling, the next challenge is assuring that acolytes arrive on the right dates, on time, ready to serve. Publishing the acolyte service schedule in the parish newsletter and Sunday bulletins, or posting it in the church is enough for some acolytes and their families, but not for others. Church newsletters addressed to the family may be shared among all family members, but sometimes not. Even when dealing with young people and children, the best bet is to send scheduling information to the individual as well as to the family. A monthly schedule published in the monthly newsletter alerts the family (and hopefully the acolyte). Adding a follow-up postcard or email addressed to the individual is inexpensive insurance and helps ensure that busy children, teens, and adults personally get scheduling information and can add it to busy calendars.

For a simple postcard, set up a fill-in-the blank postcard format on your word processing program, and print four postcards at a time on postcard stock that can be purchased at any office supply store. To save even more time, print ten or fifteen sheets at a time. Turn the sheets over and print the return address on the other side (or have them printed at a local copy shop). When schedules are completed each month, simply write in the names and dates on individual postcards, stick an address label to the front, stamp, and mail. As an alternative, you can buy index paper at most office supply stores and cut your own postcards. A single postcard might look like this:

Sample Reminder Postcard

Dear _____

This just a reminder that you are scheduled to serve as an acolyte on _____ at the _____ service.

Please don't forget to arrive at least 15 minutes early (20 minutes for crucifers).

If you have a schedule conflict, it is your responsibility to find a replacement. If you cannot find a replacement, please contact me at 555-2525.

Thank you for serving!

(signed) _____, Acolyte Leader

More postcard examples are included at the end of this chapter.

Keeping Track

Having an up-to-date acolyte roster allows you, the parish staff, and the acolytes themselves to schedule, coordinate replacements, or pass messages as needed. However, those same rosters can provide information to outsiders that your acolytes and their families may not want released. Following is an easy format that can be used for an in-house roster (for yourself and your parish secretary) and contains the information you need for scheduling, mailings, and keeping track of training. A separate abbreviated format can be given to acolytes so that they find replacements for themselves when they can't serve as scheduled. This roster should be part of every acolyte's personal manual. See the sample on pages 60–61. Since acolytes join, leave, and train for new positions, it's important to send out updated copies at least once or twice a year.

A simple roster on a word processing program can be updated and copied onto several different files (one with addresses, one without, and one for use as a checklist and so forth). This also allows you to use the rosters for different management chores. A word processing program with a table function (although not strictly necessary) allows you to easily drop address or phone columns and add scheduling columns or whatever you need. For example, a master roster might contain:

Sample Roster

T = Torchbearer	Th = Thurifer	S = Server
C = Crucifer	B = Banner bearer	

Trained for	Name/family name if different	Address	Phone #/email
T/C/S	Carry A. Candle (Nolte)	12 Acolyte Lane Wayfair, PA 16345	(717) 333-1212 cerryc@noname.com

For a scheduling roster, you can drop the addresses and add a "last scheduled" column. For tracking which acolytes will be available for a special event, drop the address column, and add a yes/no column. The same information can be maintained on a data base program if you are familiar with those programs and find it useful. Conversely, you can type or write a column of names on a plain sheet of paper, copy it several times, and draw in the extra columns with a ruler, as you need them. The only real question is which you find easiest and least time-consuming to work with. More sample rosters are provided at the end of this chapter.

Budgeting and Reimbursement

Vestments wear out, equipment needs to be repaired, brass needs to be resealed every two to three years, and training needs to be done routinely. Many acolyte programs are underfunded partially because the vestry and clergy don't understand the expenses or have any idea what current prices are for vestments, books, equipment, and so on. The best way to ensure that money is available when you need it is to submit a complete and well-researched budget. Arranging expenses into categories and listing specific items, prices, and even supply sources when possible, makes it obvious that you've done your homework, and increases the likelihood that your request will be funded. You can't predict every contingency, but acolyte programs, no matter the size, have some standard operating costs.

To begin a budget, it's helpful to look at past program costs. Ask the parish administrator or treasurer for copies of past budgets as well as a listing of actual bills paid by the church in the last three to five years for the acolyte program. Using this information, make an initial list of expenses.

One of the most frequently listed items on acolyte budgets is vestment repair and replacement. If the parish keeps a range of vestments on hand, note size gaps, and add the purchase of missing vestments to your list. Check for vestments that have been repaired more than once, as they are the ones most likely to need replacing in the coming year. If the parish assigns vestments to individual acolytes, make a point of checking the vestments as acolytes serve, and note any that need to be repaired or replaced.

Add the services that may have been donated in the past to your list. For example, in some parishes, a volunteer handles laundering and mending vestments or equipment repairs. However, if that person is no longer able or willing to donate those services, the expense may have to come out of the budget at commercial prices. Adding donated services also shows the vestry that you have considered the possible expense.

Another source of information is your parish priest. Ask specifically about any special services, events, or changes in serving routine he or she is considering so you can plan for extra equipment or supplies that may be needed. Ask the priest also to suggest any expenses you might have overlooked or of which you might not be aware.

Once you have an expense list, the next step is gathering information to estimate costs. Church catalogs are a good resource for pricing vestments and equipment as long as you don't forget to add shipping to the listed price of the item. Another resource is the parish treasurer or secretary who can often provide copies of past receipts and the names of local repair shops for estimates on equipment repairs.

Another reason for asking for past budgets is to copy the formatting. Once you have the budget formatted, it can be kept on a word processing directory or a separate disk and simply updated in the future. A sample budget is shown below.

Sample Budget

Acolyte Budget Request for 20XX

Postage		
Scheduling cards, letters, etc.		$ 33.00
Acolyte training		120.00
Copying	8.00	
Manuals ($14 each)	112.00	
Annual Acolyte Festival		267.00
Registration	170.00	
Van rental and gas	97.00	
Vestments		
Laundering/mending		(Donated)
Replace 2 worn albs (CM Almy)		128.00
Re-brass and repair torches		128.00
(estimate from All Brass, Inc.)		
Thank-you gifts for departing acolytes		60.00
TOTAL REQUEST:		$736.00

The vestry may or may not approve the full amount of your request. If not, you may need to decide on priorities and move some of the purchases or repairs into the next year or look for other funding.

Once the vestry has approved the budget, it's important to track how it's spent. Your original price estimates may be billed at slightly more or less than you anticipated. Unexpected requirements during the year, such as equipment repairs, can also change your priorities. To create a budget-tracking sheet, simply copy the budget onto another word processing file (or a plain sheet of paper) and add columns for expenses and notes. A budget-tracking sheet helps you control spending and make decisions about unexpected expenses as you go through the year. See the sample tracking sheet on page 64.

To purchase small items such as postage stamps, it's sometimes easier to buy it yourself and request reimbursement rather than request a check one to two weeks in advance. Having a simple, fill-in-the-blank letter format in a file folder or on a computer file allows you to add the name, price, and purpose of the item you purchased, attach a receipt, and mail. See the sample at the end of this chapter. In place of a lost receipt, most churches will accept a short statement explaining the loss, where you purchased the item, and the cost.

Annual Vestry Report

The vestry's annual summary, with its collection of attached committee and ministry reports, tells both parish members and the diocese how well we, as a church, used our resources and met the objectives set at the beginning of the year. Resources include money collected as alms each Sunday or through fund-raising or donations, donations of supplies and equipment, and definitely our time. As a ministry chair, therefore, your report needs to include what resources your program used, how they were used, and how your program supported the parish mission and objectives. The best reports are generally short, simple and to the point.

Specific and useful information includes the number of acolytes serving, the number of hours of support they provided, the special services they supported during the year, accomplishments in training, the number of acolytes who trained for new positions (goes towards next year's support), and how the program supported the goals or objectives of the parish or diocese. The following is provided as an example:

Sample Annual Report

Your Name
Address

Church Name
Address

Date: _____

In the past year, twenty-three acolytes contributed approximately 354 volunteer hours in support of parish worship services. Five acolytes moved to other ministries or graduated from high school and moved to other parishes. Six new acolytes joined the program. Achievements for the year included refining general procedures for festival and community services, which supports the parish objective to spread the love of God in the community. We purchased new acolyte manuals to help improve our service on the altar and to the parish. We also developed a new reward program for years of service with a separate reward for acolytes leaving our parish. Both meet the objective of encouraging continued lay service. We thank Mrs. Kathy Smith for donating her time to mend and clean vestments. This saved enough money in the budget for us to purchase several new vestments and solve the problem of a gap in sizes.

Yours in Service,

(Signed)
Your Name
Acolyte Leader

Other Paperwork

Having the routine management and administrative paperwork clearly labeled on a separate disk or directory, or a separate paper file so that you don't have to recreate it every time the need arises, cuts the work by half. You still need to gather information to update budgets and reports but don't need to format and retype. Collecting samples of paperwork and formats used by your predecessors or other acolyte leaders is also helpful and means you don't have to create reports from scratch. It's important to understand that each piece of paperwork has a real purpose (and to understand that purpose) but not to let creating your own versions take up more time than it deserves.

Sample Forms

Samples you can use in building your own forms, formats, and management tools are on the following pages. Spend a few minutes adapting these for your parish, and cut operating chores down to size.

Scheduling Worksheets

Following are sample worksheets for a routine monthly and Easter/Holy Week schedule. Use one copy to plan, scribble notes, and confirm participants, and then write the final schedule onto a clean copy and hand or email it to church staff.

Monthly Schedule

Date	Service needs	Other family members involved in this service	Confirmed? Card or call
Dec 7	_____ A.M. Service _____ Server _____ _____	Ushers? LEM/Chalice? Nursery?	
	_____ A.M. Service Server _____ Crucifer _____ Torchbearer _____ Torchbearer _____		
Dec 14	_____ A.M. Service Server _____		
	_____ A.M. Service Server _____ Crucifer _____ Torchbearer _____ Torchbearer _____		
Dec 21	_____ A.M. Service Server _____		
	_____ A.M. Service Server _____ Crucifer _____ Torchbearer _____ Torchbearer _____		
Dec 28	_____ A.M. Service Server _____		
	_____ A.M. Service Server _____ Crucifer _____ Torchbearer _____ Torchbearer _____		

Easter Week

Services	Ph.	Alternates	Other family involved	Confirmed
Maundy Thursday _____ P.M. Server _____ Crucifer _____ Torch _____ Torch _____			Ushers? Greeters? Lem? Nursery?	
Good Friday _____ A.M. Server/Crucifer _____				
Good Friday _____ P.M. Server _____				
Easter Vigil _____ P.M. Server _____ Crucifer _____				
Easter Sunday _____ A.M. Server _____ Crucifer _____ Torch _____ Torch _____				
Easter Festival _____ A.M. Thurifer _____ Boat _____ Lead crucifer _____ Torch _____ Torch _____ Book _____ Banner _____ Clergy crucifer _____ Torch _____ Torch _____ Server _____ Senior acolyte _____				

Roster #1
Master Acolyte Roster

Date: _____

T = Torch   Th = Thurifer
C = Crucifer   B = Banner bearer   S = Server

Trained as	Name	Address	Phone #/email
T/C/S	Carry A. Candle (Nolte)	12 Acolyte Lane Wayfair, PA 16345	(717) 333-1212 cerryc@noname.com

Acolyte Leader _____ Phone# _____
email_____
Assistant Leader _____ Phone# _____
email_____

Roster #2
This is a simple roster that can be handed out to each acolyte

Acolyte Roster

Date: _____

Acolytes—You are responsible for finding your own replacement if you can't serve as scheduled. If you can't find a replacement, please call the scheduled server or the acolyte leader as soon as possible!
PLEASE do NOT share this roster or the information on it with others.

T = Torch   B = Banner bearer
C = Crucifer   Th = Thurifer
S = Server

Trained as	Name	Phone #/email
T/C/S	Carry A. Candle	unlisted carryc@noname.com

Please call if you have questions or need help.

Acolyte Leader _____ Phone# _____

email_____

Roster #3

Scheduling Roster

Date: _____

T = Torch
C = Crucifer
S = Server
B = Banner bearer
Th = Thurifer

Trained as	Name	Phone #/email	Sequence number	Last scheduled?
T/C/S	Carry A. Candle	unlisted carryc@noname.com		

Sample Postcards

The notices below fit on the back of a standard 3.5 x 4.5-inch postcard. Four copies of the notice will fit on each sheet of computer postcard stock or a standard sheet of heavy index paper turned sideways. The difference between postcard stock and index paper is that postcard stock is perforated so you can tear postcards apart rather than use a ruler and office paper cutter. It also costs considerably more. Print a supply of cards, fill in the extra information, put an address label and stamp on the front, and mail.

Postcard #1 —Scheduling

Dear _____
This is just a reminder that you are scheduled to serve as an acolyte on
_____ at the _____ service.

Please don't forget to arrive at 15 minutes early (20 minutes for crucifers).

If you have a schedule conflict, it is your responsibility to find a replacement. If you cannot find a replacement, please contact me at 333-4444.

Thank you for serving!
(Signed) _____, Acolyte Leader

Postcard #2—Training Announcement

Dear _____

Acolyte training is scheduled for Sunday, Nov. 15 after the family service. The session will last approximately one hour.

Training includes new acolytes and I'll need your help as a mentor or trainer for that. This is also an opportunity for you to brush up or train for a new position, if you like. We will also briefly walk-though the upcoming holiday services.

Please plan to be there on Nov. 15.
Thank you for serving!

(Signed) _____, Acolyte Leader

Annual Acolyte Program Budget

Here's a sample format you can use as a basis to prepare your own budget.

FROM:
Name
Address
Phone Number

TO:
Treasurer
Church Name
Address

Date: _____

Acolyte budget request for the year _____

Postage		
Scheduling cards, letters, etc.		$ 33.00
Acolyte training		120.00
Copying	8.00	
Manuals ($14 each)	112.00	
Annual Acolyte Festival		267.00
Registration	170.00	
Van rental and gas	97.00	
Vestments		
Laundering/mending		(Donated)
Replace 2 worn albs (CM Almy)		128.00
Re-brass and repair torches		125.00
(estimate from All Brass, Inc.)		
Thank-you gifts for departing acolytes		60.00
TOTAL REQUEST:		$733.00

Thank you for your support of the Acolyte Program.

Sincerely,

(signed)

Acolyte Leader

Sample Budget Tracking Sheet

A budget tracking worksheet is a simple way to keep track of the funds during the year. One easy way to do this is to copy the budget onto another word processing file or plain sheet of paper and add columns for actual expenses and notes.

Sample acolyte budget tracking for the year _____

Budgeted		Spent/date	Notes
Postage			Postcard
Scheduling cards, letters, etc.	33.00	23.00 Feb 1	stamps
Acolyte Training	120.00	3.50 Mar 10	Copy Shop
Copying 8.00		$101.40 Apr 2	7 new manuals
Manuals (Morehouse, 14.00 each) 112.00			plus postage
Annual Acolyte Festival	267.00	120.00 Sep 6	12 acolytes,
Registration $170.00			1 priest
Van rental and gas $ 97.00		$98.50 Oct 12	Van/gas
Vestments			
Laundering/mending	Donated)		Sizes 55 & 57
Replace 2 worn albs (CM Almy)	128.00	136.00 Jun 3	plus postage
Re-brass and repair Torches	125.00	142.50 May 6	New staffs were
(estimate from All Brass, Inc.)			also required
Thank-you gifts for departing acolytes	60.00	46.00 May 15	5 sun catchers
		Subtotal	The Glass Shop
		($670.00)	
ADDED:			
Replace chain and repair thurible_____		58.50 Sep 12	Chain broke and
_____			thurible hit pew
_____			during practice
_____			
TOTAL REQUEST $790.00		As of Dec 1	
		(728.50)	

Sample Reimbursement Request

Leaving the underlined portion blank, make several paper copies or type this format into a word processing file. When you purchase something, simply write or type in the item, purpose, and cost. Attach the receipt and mail.

Your name
Address
Phone number

Church name
Address

Date: _____

Request for Reimbursement:

   I request reimbursement for <u>postcard stock and stamps</u>. These are used <u>to mail out reminders for acolytes on the service schedule</u>.

The receipt is attached. Thank you.

Sincerely,

(Signed)

Your Name
Acolyte Leader

Enclosure
Receipt dated: _____

Resources for Acolytes Leaders

Published literature for acolyte leaders is relatively scarce, sometimes dated, and seldom written for use by lay people. There are, however, some excellent books, most still in print, that contain related information useful to acolytes and acolyte leaders.

The most valuable resource for acolyte leaders is the 1979 Book of Common Prayer. Having your own working copy in which you can highlight specific rubrics, write notes, tab pages, and leave sticky notes is a real asset. Two other valuable books include *A Priest's Handbook*, by the Reverend Dennis G. Michno (also author of *A Manual for Acolytes: The Duties of the Server at Liturgical Celebrations*), and *The Ceremonies of the Eucharist* by Howard E. Galley. Without a theological background, you may need your parish priest to interpret some sections, but the wealth of information is well worth the effort.

Surprisingly, there are also some useful resources available on the world wide web. The Cathedral of the King website (www.iccec-sea.org/liturgy) includes easily accessible and readable answers for almost any question about vestments and equipment used in the church. The Lambeth Palace Library website (Lambethpalacelibrary.org/holdings/guides/#liturgical) is also useful if you're interested in historical information on clerical wear and vestments. And for a fast, down-to-earth, answer on Episcopalian terminology, check the Reverend John Burwell's glossary on the Holy Cross website (www.holycross.net/anonline.htm).

Some General Resources

The Episcopal Church. The Book of Common Prayer. New York: The Church Hymnal Corp., 1979.

Galley, Howard E. *The Ceremonies of the Eucharist: A Guide to Celebration.* Cambridge, Mass.: Cowley Publications, 1989.

Heller, Christopher. *The New Complete Server.* Harrisburg, Pa.: Morehouse Publishing, 1995.

Hickman, Hoyt L. *The Acolyte's Book.* Nashville, Tenn.: Abingdon Press, 1985.

Michno, Dennis. *A Manual for Acolytes: The Duties of the Server at Liturgical Celebrations.* Wilton, Conn.: Morehouse-Barlow Co., 1981.

Michno, Dennis G. *A Priest's Handbook: The Ceremonies of the Church, 3rd ed.* Harrisburg, Pa.: Morehouse Publishing, 1998.

Price, Charles P. and Weil, Louis. *Liturgy for Living*. Harrisburg, Pa.: Morehouse Publishing, 2000.

The Episcopal Church. The Book of Occasional Services. New York: Church Publishing Corp., 1994.

Stuhlman, Bryan D. *The Prayer Book Rubrics Expanded*. New York: The Church Hymnal Corp., 1987.

Resources on Acolyte History

Grun, Bernard. *The Timetables of History: The New Third Revised Edition*. New York: Simon and Schuster, 1991.

The Catholic Encyclopedia, 1999 online edition. s.v. "Acolyte."

Encyclopedia of the Lutheran Church, 1999 ed., s.v. "Acolyte."

The New Catholic Encyclopedia, Thomson/Gale, Detroit, in association with the Catholic University, Washington, DC. 2002. s.v. "Altar Server."

"The History of the Office Of Acolytes." The Trinity Lutheran Church website: www.tlc3n1.org/acolyte.html. 2002.